SPORT HYPNOSIS

DONALD R. LIGGETT, PHD

HUMAN KINETICS

Library of Congress Cataloging-in-Publication Data

Liggett, Donald R., 1923-
    Sport hypnosis / Donald R. Liggett.
      p. cm.
    Includes bibliographical references (p.) and index.
    ISBN 0-7360-0214-6
    1. Sports--Psychological aspects. 2. Hypnotism. I. Title.
    GV706.4 L56 2000
796'.01--dc21   99-050149

ISBN: 0-7360-0214-6
Copyright © 2000 by Donald R. Liggett

Developmental Editors: Amy N. Pickering and Julie A. Marx; **Assistant Editors:** Amy Flaig and Stephan Seyfert; **Copyeditor:** Denelle Eknes; **Proofreader:** Julie A. Marx; **Indexer:** Daniel A. Connolly; **Permission Manager:** Cheri Banks; **Graphic Designer:** Nancy Rasmus; **Graphic Artist:** Tara Welsch; **Photo Editor:** Clark Brooks; **Cover Designer:** Keith Blomberg; **Photographer (cover):** Tom Roberts; **Photographer (interior):** Tom Roberts unless otherwise noted; photo on page 2 courtesy of Dr. Sybil Eysenck; photos on pages 40, 42, 43, 101, 130, and 152 courtesy of Dr. Donald R. Liggett; photo on page 166 © Brian Spurlock/Joe Robbins Photography; **Illustrator:** Craig Newsom; **Printer:** Versa Press

Human Kinetics books are available at special discounts for bulk purchase. Special editions or book excerpts can also be created to specification. For details, contact the Special Sales Manager at Human Kinetics.

Printed in the United States of America   10 9 8 7 6 5 4 3 2 1

Human Kinetics
Web site: http://www.humankinetics.com/

United States: Human Kinetics, P.O. Box 5076, Champaign, IL 61825-5076
1-800-747-4457
e-mail: humank@hkusa.com

Canada: Human Kinetics, 475 Devonshire Road Unit 100, Windsor, ON N8Y 2L5
1-800-465-7301 (in Canada only)
e-mail: humank@hkcanada.com

Europe: Human Kinetics, P.O. Box IW14, Leeds LS16 6TR, United Kingdom
+44 (0)113-278 1708
e-mail: humank@hkeurope.com

Australia: Human Kinetics, 57A Price Avenue, Lower Mitcham, South Australia 5062
(08) 82771555
e-mail: liahka@senet.com.au

New Zealand: Human Kinetics, P.O. Box 105-231, Auckland Central
09-523-3462
e-mail: humank@hknewz.com

To my wife, Jeanne, and son, Keith,
who, while claiming to already have looked over 7,000
versions, were still willing to contribute helpful content
and style comments on the 7,007th draft.

CONTENTS

PREFACE

The room is crowded, people are laughing hysterically, and you cannot help but join the laughter. It is not every day that you see your friend standing on a chair, quacking like a duck on command in front of a large crowd. Between laughs, you make a mental note to avoid being hypnotized at all costs.

In this situation, hypnotists are showing off their cleverness at the expense of the persons they hypnotize. This use of hypnosis gives the technique a cheap carnival or shady reputation. The prospect of being used in this way is clearly not attractive.

Too many people in sports know hypnotism only from this public view. They see a hypnotist taking control of a person to exploit that person—to make volunteers from the audience do ridiculous and embarrassing acts. This does not make serious athletes interested in being hypnotized, nor do these performances suggest that a hypnotist could empower them to improve their performance.

The other side of hypnotism is less known. It is therapists and physicians using the power of hypnotism to help people overcome psychological or medical problems.

Although using hypnosis in medicine and psychotherapy is now officially recognized by medical, dental, and psychiatric associations, there is little recognition, and even less use, of its ability to empower athletes.

This book explores the constructive side of hypnosis—specifically how hypnosis can effectively empower athletes. Part I presents an overview of mental training and hypnosis, with attention to the characteristics of hypnosis that can enhance mental training.

Part II presents information on how hypnosis can enhance several aspects of mental training. Each chapter describes a skill component of mental training, its importance to an athlete, and the way hypnosis enhances the power of that technique. Included are the ways in which hypnosis helps an athlete receive more benefit from relaxation, imagery, and goal setting and how hypnosis increases control of performance arousal, concentration, pain, and healing. In exploring these topics, the book presents examples of successful applications of each technique, along with research demonstrating the value of the strategies. Included are examples drawn from the literature, from fellow sport psychologists, and from my personal experience with participants in many sports. The examples include a variety of ability levels to show how hypnotism can benefit all athletes at any level who want to improve.

Although part II isolates various mental skills, in most situations a therapist blends several techniques to empower an athlete. Thus, part III describes in detail how to apply and combine hypnotic techniques when working with athletes. Working with a young quarterback involved helping with arousal control, imagery, and goal setting. Other case studies include helping a pole-vaulter increase his vaulting height; a wild-water kayaker deepen imagery experiences with hypnosis to improve his technique; a soccer player eliminate a long-standing, debilitating hamstring pain; and a basketball player achieve a higher free throw percentage. Throughout the book, the case studies range from young athletes through high school and university athletes to elite Olympic and professional competitors.

The appendix includes a detailed script showing how you can overcome the reluctance of some athletes to use hypnosis through educating them and demystifying the technique for them.

I am excited by hypnosis' effectiveness, and I hope this book will inspire more people to benefit from the extra mental edge that hypnosis can provide. View the examples not as exact prescriptions, but as starting points. Working with athletes has always allowed—actually required—creativity from coaches and psychologists. This is particularly true with using hypnosis. Take these examples as starting points and be creative in developing your own ways of using hypnosis to improve performance.

Whether you are an athlete, a coach, or a sport psychologist, this book will help you achieve your mental training goals. It will show you how you can use hypnosis to enhance the skills you already have and gain the skills you don't have.

Acknowledgments

Many friends have helped in developing this book. Were I to list them all, the extra paper would require cutting down another tree, and I don't wish to be that ecologically destructive. Rather than listing these major and minor contributors here, their names live on in the case studies. I do this to protect not only my innocent clients but also my innocent helpers. When I use a first and last name in a case study, the identification with that person is real and that person has approved. When I use only a first name, it is likely a tribute to someone who has greatly helped me in this book—by correcting errors, by suggesting additions, or by encouraging me as I put it together. Their help has improved the book and I am grateful, but the responsibility for any errors is, of course, all mine.

PART I

INCORPORATING HYPNOSIS INTO MENTAL TRAINING

Developing mental skills is increasingly recognized as an important part of an athlete's training. It is no longer necessary to rely on chance as the source of a relaxed, confident performance. Getting into one's zone can be brought under the athlete's control. Hypnosis is gradually being used by sport psychologists, coaches, and athletes to accelerate mental training. Chapter 1 presents the characteristics of a hypnotic trance that are of use in mental training. Chapter 2 introduces how hypnosis can assist in developing the mental skills that empower an athletic performance.

Hans Jürgen Eysenck, 1916-1997

HYPNOSIS IS ONE OF THE MOST FASCINATING YET
LEAST EXPLORED PHENOMENON IN PSYCHOLOGY.

HANS EYSENCK, BRITISH PSYCHOLOGIST

Chapter 1
Demystifying Hypnosis

Although hypnosis has fascinated and mystified people for thousands of years, scientists still do not agree about the exact physiological and psychological nature of a trance or why people behave differently in a trance than out of a trance. Despite varying theoretical explanations of hypnosis, the characteristics of a person in a trance are agreed upon.

Origins of Hypnosis

Evidence of hypnotic-like phenomena appears in many ancient cultures. The writer of Genesis seems familiar with the anesthetic power of hypnosis when he reports that God put Adam "into a deep sleep" to take his rib to form Eve. Other ancient records suggest hypnosis was used by the oracle at Delphi and in rites in ancient Egypt (Hughes & Rothovius, 1996). The modern history of hypnosis begins in the late 1700s, when a French physician, Anton Mesmer, revived an interest in hypnosis. He effected many medical and psychiatric cures with an elaborate and flamboyant ritual using hypnotism—he called it animal magnetism. His successes offended the medical establishment of the time, who arranged for an official French government investigating committee. This committee included Benjamin Franklin, then the American ambassador to France, and Joseph Guillotin, a French physician who introduced a never-fail device for physically separating the mind from the rest of the body. This investigating committee declared Mesmer's claims to be fraudulent; his cures were not caused by his animal magnetism. For Paris, Mesmer's career and hypnotism itself were at an end, at least temporarily. One lasting contribution of this pioneer was the term mesmerism, an early and still-used term for hypnotism.

Medical Applications in the 1800s

In the early 1800s, several British physicians explored the use of hypnosis in healing and as an anesthetic in surgery. As ether and other chemical anesthetics came into use in the middle of the 1800s, interest in using hypnosis as an anesthetic in surgery fell off almost completely. The official medical establishment has always been slow to recognize the effectiveness of hypnosis. This was true for Mesmer, for the British physicians, and is true to some extent for athletes and coaches today.

Hypnosis Today

In the past several decades, there has been a revival of interest in hypnosis. Although the sports world has not used hypnosis extensively, other professions have recognized the contribution that hypnosis can make to their fields. In 1957, the American Medical Association adopted a policy statement recognizing hypnosis as a useful and legitimate treatment in both medicine and dentistry. The British Medical Society had done this two years earlier (Crasilneck & Hall, 1985). Hypnosis has long been a staple treatment in psychotherapy. Although today hypnosis has an established place in medicine, dentistry, and psychotherapy, in sports it is often regarded as irregular and a little suspicious. However, its use is expanding—sometimes openly, but frequently under the guise of relaxation, guided imagery, or visualization. The Executive Committee of the American Psychological Association, Division of Psychological Hypnosis, has prepared its own definition of hypnosis.

DEFINING HYPNOSIS

Hypnosis is a procedure during which a health professional or researcher suggests that a client, patient, or subject experiences changes in sensations, perceptions, thoughts, or behavior. The hypnotic context is generally established by an induction procedure. Although there are many different hypnotic inductions, most include suggestions for relaxation, calmness, and well-being. Instructions to imagine or think about pleasant experiences are also commonly included in hypnotic inductions. People respond to hypnosis in different ways. Some describe their experience as an altered state of consciousness. Others describe hypnosis as a normal state of focused attention, in which they feel very calm and relaxed. Regardless of how and to what degree they respond, most people describe the experience as very pleasant.

Some people are very responsive to hypnotic suggestions, and others are less responsive. A person's ability to experience hypnotic suggestions can be inhibited by fears and concerns arising from some common misconceptions. Contrary to some depictions of hypnosis in books, movies, or on television, people who have been hypnotized do not lose control over their behavior. They typically remain aware of who they are and where they are, and unless amnesia has been specifically suggested, they usually remember what transpired during hypnosis. Hypnosis makes it easier for people to experience suggestions, but it does not force them to have these experiences.

Hypnosis is not a type of therapy, like psychoanalysis or behavior therapy. Instead, it is a procedure that can be used to facilitate therapy. Because it is not a treatment in and of itself, training in hypnosis is not sufficient for the conduct of therapy. Clinical hypnosis should be used only by properly trained and credentialed health care professionals (e.g., licensed clinical psychologists) who have also been trained in the clinical use of hypnosis and are working within the areas of their professional expertise.

Hypnosis has been used in the treatment of pain, depression, anxiety, stress, habit disorders, and many other psychological and medical problems. However, it may not be useful for all psychological problems or for all patients or clients. The decision to use hypnosis as an adjunct to treatment can only be made in consultation with a qualified health care provider who has been trained in the use and limitations of clinical hypnosis. In addition to its use in clinical settings, hypnosis is used in research, with the goal of learning more about the nature of hypnosis itself, as well as its impact on sensation, perception, learning, memory, and physiology. Researchers also study the value of hypnosis in the treatment of physical and psychological problems.

This definition and description of hypnosis was prepared by the Executive Committee of the American Psychological Association, Division of Psychological Hypnosis. Permission to reproduce this information is freely granted.

Trance Debate

Some psychologists doubt that there is any reality to the concept of a trance. They point out that scientists have found no physiological way to determine whether a person is in a trance. They also emphasize that persons who are not in a trance can duplicate many characteristics of a trance. They claim that the person in a trance is behaving according to the same behavioral principles that apply to persons in the normal waking state.

Other psychologists believe that a hypnotic trance is an altered state of consciousness. In my experience, a person in a trance behaves differently than when out of a trance. To those who have watched stage hypnotists, it certainly appears that people do act differently in a trance.

The behaviors characteristic of a person in a trance are of more interest here than the exact physiological nature of the trance state. For an in-depth discussion of a trance physiology and psychology, see Hughes and Rothovius (1996) and Kirsch and Lynn (1995).

Nature of a Trance

Superficially, persons in a trance may look as though they are asleep, but a hypnotic trance is different from a coma or sleep. Possibly the most important differences are that a person in a trance, although usually relaxed, is aware of the environment, will respond to suggestions from the hypnotist, and usually can later remember what transpired in the trance.

A trance is not like an on-off switch. People enter a trance gradually, and they experience different levels of a trance. Although we talk about being in or out of a trance, the trance state is much more like a continuum than a dichotomy. Being in a trance usually means that the person is deep enough to accept some suggestions.

Trance Depth

The frequently used terms level and depth need some definition. A person in a deeper level of trance is more likely to accept suggestions than one in a less deep trance, or out of a trance. In simple terms, the deeper you are in a trance, the more susceptible you are to suggestions. Some people can achieve a deep level easily; some achieve a deep level only after several sessions, and some never get very deep. I have found that most of what I want to achieve in a trance can be realized when a person is not very deep, that is, in a light trance, and only rarely is a deeper level necessary.

Hypnotic Susceptibility

Some similarity exists between the depth of trance individuals can achieve and their score on the standard tests of hypnotic susceptibility. The two most used tests of hypnotic susceptibility are the Stanford Hypnotic Susceptibility Scale (Weitzenhoffer & Hilgard, 1959) and the Harvard Group Scale of Hypnotic Susceptibility (Shor & Orne, 1962). The Stanford scale is individually administered, and the Harvard scale is a group test based on the Stanford Scale. Your susceptibility score on either the Harvard or Stanford scales is the number of suggestions that you accept after a standardized hypnotic induction. In general then, the more susceptible you are to hypnosis, the deeper you will go with a standard induction, and the deeper the trance, the greater the probability of accepting suggestions.

Some therapists test susceptibility before working with athletes. However, it is more efficient to assume that people are sufficiently hypnotizable. Because the standard tests of susceptibility take about an hour, using one merely delays constructive work.

WORKING TOGETHER

If an athlete and I are able to achieve a trance, then we can begin work. (I use "we" here because hypnosis is a cooperative venture between two people—not something one person does to another.) If we do not achieve a trance, we can decide to try later, or we can work with some other method of mental training. I have found that fewer than 1 out of 20 athletes is not susceptible, so I rarely use tests of susceptibility.

However, when doing research on hypnosis, this procedure is not appropriate because one usually must cite the hypnotizability of the participants in a study.

Characteristics of a Trance

Athletes can use many characteristics of the hypnotic trance to benefit their performances. We have all experienced these characteristics to some extent without a trance. In a trance state however, they are more pronounced.

• **Relaxation.** It is appropriate to mention relaxation first because it is the most noticeable characteristic of a trance. When a person comes out of a trance, the relaxation of the body and the mind is the most common sensation. While in a trance, this relaxation allows a variety of treatments. The relaxation experienced in a trance has some superficial resemblance to sleep, and thus, the name hypnosis, from *Hypnos,* the Greek god of sleep. A hypnotic trance is different from sleep—the relaxation being the most obvious but about the only similarity.

• **Suggestibility.** When people think of hypnosis, the most prominent characteristic is the willingness of the subject to accept suggestions. Anyone who has watched a stage hypnotist has seen the power of the suggestions the hypnotist makes. Although these stage suggestions are seldom any help to the person hypnotized, this book shows how hypnotic suggestions can be used to empower athletes.

This suggestibility is often misunderstood. A hypnotized person retains an important degree of control and can resist suggestions as well as follow them. It is generally believed that people will not perform acts or accept ideas that are against their moral or physical well-being, though this belief is difficult to test ethically. How can you conduct an ethical experiment in which the experimenter asks participants to do things that violate their ethical or physical well-being? If participants are not asked to do these things, how can the study demonstrate that they won't behave unethically or in ways that could be damaging?

• **Concentration.** A person in a trance has an increased ability to focus or concentrate, which is appealing to athletes. It is possible for a hypnotized person to ignore distractions in the surroundings and to zero in on feelings, on specific stimuli, or on a past or imagined event. This focus is in some ways similar to our mental state when we are watching a movie and are totally focused on—absorbed in—the action on the screen. At such times we are oblivious of anything except the action on the screen.

Likewise, the ability to focus on a past event has been helpful to athletes. The details available in a trance enable one to relive a past event and to analyze the factors contributing to the success or failure much more clearly than otherwise. This ability to focus accurately on a past event has also been useful in forensic work. A witness to an accident or crime can in a trance often recall details that are not available in the usual conscious state.

DRIVING IN A HYPNOTIC STATE

Many of us have experienced something similar to this focused hypnotic state when driving a car. When we are familiar with a route, driving to work for example, we travel the route automatically. We might even catch ourselves having used this automatic pilot—we arrive at home and realize we completely forgot to pick up that quart of milk.

• **Imaginative ability.** In a trance a person has enhanced imaginative abilities. This imaginative power is a major problem in forensic work. The imagination of the hypnotized person can (and often does) fill in gaps in what was observed. Thus a description of an earlier event includes recollections plus imagined details for other aspects. The hypnotized person is generally unable to separate the recalled from the imagined—both seem equally real. This can be a problem when an athlete recalls a previous performance. The event may be recalled in great detail, but the description will include an indeterminate number of details that are not true.

• **Reality testing.** This imaginative power also enables the subject to reduce current reality testing—to accept distortions of time, cognition, and affect, for example. Logical inconsistencies can be easily accepted. This characteristic is how the stage hypnotist makes subjects see things that are not there, feel they are in a different place, or behave as a different type of person. Similarly, this ability to distort time helps a diver or gymnast to vividly rehearse a dive or trick in slow motion.

SEEING THE STORY

We often experience this imaginative ability, and hypnotic-like state, when we are entranced by reading an exciting book and can see the scene and people of the story.

• **Brain function.** A hypnotic trance allows access to different functions of the brain. This characteristic is particularly valuable to psychotherapists. Two different aspects of mind functions are of interest here. Sigmund Freud, the founder of psychoanalysis, proposed an unconscious mind, where we bury many of our motivations and past experiences—inaccessible to our conscious mind. The motivations, though inaccessible to the conscious mind, are powerful determinants of our behavior. These unconscious motivations are more accessible in a trance than otherwise. Understanding unconscious motivations is a major concern of a psychotherapist and is frequently a help in working with athletes.

Another theory suggests that the two halves of the brain have differing functions. The left brain provides the logical, rational thinking about details, while the right brain is the emotional side and is cognizant of overall organization—the gestalt of a situation. Hypnosis allows more access to the qualities associated with the right brain. Tapping into both is particularly valuable in psychotherapy, but is also frequently useful in the mental training of athletes. The imaginative skill of the right brain can help make hypnotic imagery sessions more vivid, and thus more powerful.

• **Autonomic control.** Another characteristic is the ability to control some autonomic functions such as blood flow and blood pressure. This aspect of hypnosis is more frequently used in medicine than in sports, but is often relevant to athletes. This control is important in facilitating recovery from injuries. With an increase in the flow of blood and other healing fluids to the site of an injury, recovery is more rapid. Likewise, hypnosis is valuable in pain control. This characteristic is widely recognized and has obvious applications in sports medicine.

Anxiety has both physiological and psychological aspects and its control is important. You can teach control of both aspects effectively in a trance.

• **Placebo effect.** One final characteristic of hypnosis that I must mention is the placebo effect. To most people, being hypnotized is an impressive experience. As with many treatments, if the person believes that this experience will help, the chances of its success are greatly enhanced. William Brown (1997) explained the power of the placebo effect and urged physicians and others to take more advantage of this phenomenon. For some, simply a belief that a technique will be helpful is enough to bring about the desired change. Although the placebo effect often muddies an experimental analysis of the effect of hypnosis, in practice it can make a positive contribution to the hypnosis. Even though the placebo effect may explain part of the effectiveness of hypnosis, I have found that the other characteristics of a hypnotic trance are equally important in helping athletes.

All these characteristics of hypnosis are useful from time to time while working with athletes. The uses of relaxation, suggestibility, imaginative powers, thought processes, autonomic functions, and even the placebo effect can help athletes achieve their performance goals.

Being Hypnotized

You may enter a trance either by working with another person, which is called hetero-hypnosis, or you can induce a trance yourself without the aid of another person, which is called self-hypnosis. Although a self-induced trance is usually not as deep as a hetero-induced trance, much of what you can accomplish by hetero-hypnosis you can achieve by self-hypnosis.

The easiest way to learn self-hypnosis is from the person who helped to hetero-induce the trance. It is possible to learn self-hypnosis without help from a hypnotist, but this is difficult for most people. There are books on this topic, but I have found few people who have learned to self-induce a deep trance without the help of a qualified hypnotist. I am sure there are successes in self-instruction, because books touting this are available, but I have found that it is easier to learn this from a hypnotist than from a book. One of the best procedures for learning self-hypnosis is outlined by Nideffer (1992) in his book, *Psyched to Win*. The following example is a self-hypnosis script for tennis developed from Nideffer. You can modify this script to make it specific to your sport if you are a coach or an athlete, or to the sport you are working with if you are a sport psychologist.

SELF-HYPNOSIS SCRIPT

Phase 1

Close your eyes, and begin by taking three deep breaths. Inhale deeply, and exhale slowly. . . . Inhale deeply, and exhale slowly. . . . Inhale deeply, and exhale slowly. That's fine, . . . now just relax, let yourself go, and know that no matter how deeply hypnotized you become, you will always be in control and able to respond to anything that you choose to respond to. . . . No matter how deeply hypnotized you become, you will remember everything.

Begin to concentrate on your right arm. . . . Position your right arm so that your hand is open, and your palm is facing up. . . . That's fine. . . . Now pay attention to the feelings in your upper arm, . . . in your forearm, . . . in your hand and fingers. Notice any sensations that may be occurring in your right arm. . . . You may feel a breeze blowing across the hairs. You may feel a tingling sensation in your hand or fingers. Just observe the feelings. . . .

Now, notice the feelings of heaviness that occur in your right arm as you exhale. . . . Just relax, and notice the feeling of comfortable, relaxed, heaviness that develops in your right arm as you exhale. . . .

Take your left arm and position it so that your fingers are open, but your palm is facing down. . . . *(Repeat this sentence to give yourself time to respond.)* Make a slight bend in your left wrist. . . . Good. . . . Now, pay attention to the feelings in your left hand. Notice as you inhale how your hand begins to feel lighter. . . . Just relax, and notice as you inhale how your hand begins to feel lighter, as if it wants to lift up. . . .

You can create different feelings in your hands if you want to, all you have to do is find the right images. . . . Do that now. Pay attention to your right hand again. Find an image that helps you develop the feeling of heaviness in your right hand. Imagine that you are closing your right hand around a weight, and that the weight is pulling your hand down, making it heavier, . . . and heavier, . . . heavier, . . . and heavier. . . . Just let yourself go, and find an image that makes your right arm feel heavier and heavier with each exhalation.

That's fine. . . . Get rid of that image and let the feelings of heaviness go. . . . Now, pay attention to your left arm. Imagine a friend reaching out and taking hold of your wrist between thumb and forefinger. Imagine that each time you inhale, your friend gently tugs on your wrist, making it feel lighter . . . and lighter. . . . Each time you inhale, your friend gently tugs on your wrist pulling it higher . . . and higher, . . . making it lighter, . . . and lighter. . . . Good. Notice how much lighter your wrist has become. Find another image that will make your wrist and arm feel even lighter. . . . Take some time and develop the feelings of lightness in your left hand. . . .

ALLOW A TWO-MINUTE BREAK HERE FOR FEELINGS TO DEVELOP.

Phase 2

Good. Now just relax. If your left arm has moved, settle it back down into a comfortable position. As your arm settles down, you will feel very comfortable. . . . You can increase this pleasant, comfortable feeling by counting from one to five. . . . With each count you will become more relaxed and more deeply hypnotized. No matter how deeply hypnotized you become, however, you will always be in control. . . . With each count you will become more relaxed and more deeply hypnotized. No matter how deeply hypnotized you become, however, you will always be in control. . . .

One, . . . relax all of the muscles in both of your arms, in the fingers, . . . hands, . . . forearms, . . . and upper arms. . . . Just completely relax those muscles and enjoy the pleasant feeling of heaviness that occurs as you exhale and sink down deeper and deeper. . . .

Two, . . . relax the muscles in both legs. . . . Relax the muscles in your feet and toes. . . . Relax the muscles in your calves. . . . Relax the muscles in your thighs. . . . Just completely relax all of the muscles in both arms and both legs, and notice as you exhale . . . the pleasant sensation of drifting down deeper and deeper, . . . into a deep hypnotic state.

Three, . . . relax all of the muscles in your forehead, . . . cheeks, . . . and jaw. . . . Let your mouth open slightly as you relax the muscles in your jaw. . . . That's fine. . . .

Four, . . . relax the muscles in your neck. . . . Relax the muscles in your shoulders. . . . Just completely relax, drifting down deeper, . . . deeper, . . . still deeper. . . .

Five, . . . relax the muscles in your chest, . . . back, . . . and stomach. . . . Relax all of your muscles and enjoy the pleasant sensations of being deeply hypnotized. . . . For the next few moments just let yourself go completely, and with each exhale drift down deeper and deeper. . . . With each exhale . . . drift down deeper . . . and deeper. . . .

ALLOW A ONE-MINUTE BREAK HERE.

Phase 3 (Tennis Specific)

Now, . . . imagine that you are about to serve. . . . As you prepare to serve, look to the other side of the court. . . . You have soft eyes, . . . seeing your opponent waiting to receive the serve. At the same time, you can see the entire court. . . . You can see everything. . . . As you stand there, you decide where you will serve, . . . and you make up your mind that you are going to stay back on this point, to play from the baseline. . . .

You can feel the ball in your hand. . . . You can feel its texture and weight. . . . You can feel the seams where there isn't any fuzz. Notice the feeling of your racket in your hand as you grip it. . . . Notice how tightly you hold it. Notice how it feels against your palms . . . and your fingertips. . . .

Pay attention to your weight distribution. . . . Notice how your center of mass shifts toward your front foot as you bounce the ball and prepare to serve. . . . You feel very comfortable and balanced. . . . Now, as you begin your toss, your attention narrows and you focus on the spot where you are tossing the ball. . . . As your concentration narrows, you see the ball come into view very clearly. You can see the fuzz on the ball, . . . see its color, . . . see it rotate. . . . As you watch the ball, you can feel your racket coming through, and you see it as it comes into your field of vision. You can see it make contact with the ball, and you can feel your weight and your center of mass transferring, moving forward, coming through at the moment your racket contacts the ball. . . . Now, you feel the follow-through of your racket.

Quickly, your attention broadens again and you see the whole court. You can feel yourself recenter as you bring your legs under you. You feel balanced and centered. Your racket is up and you are ready to move in any direction. . . .

Phase 4 (Tennis Specific)

That's fine. Now just play some points so things can happen at their regular speed. . . . Let your imagination go. . . . Get completely involved in the points. . . . You will feel and see everything as if you were actually playing the points. . . . You will feel confident, . . . in control. . . . It's easy to move and to get into position, to feel your weight move through the ball with each stroke. . . . You seem to have all the time in the world to prepare. . . . You know that you can do anything you want to with the ball. . . . Just let yourself play, enjoying all of the feelings and sensations that come when you are in the zone. . . .

LEAVE TWO MINUTES HERE FOR MENTAL REHEARSAL.

Phase 5 (Tennis Specific)

That's fine. In a moment it will be time to leave this pleasant state of hypnosis. . . . Before you do, however, you need to know that you will be able to create the feelings that you have when you are playing in the zone whenever you want. . . . You will be able to do this by taking a deep, centering breath, . . . inhaling deeply, . . . and attending to the expansion of the muscles in your abdomen as you inhale. As you exhale, . . . relax your chest, neck, and shoulder muscles and say, "_____ and _____" *(insert your two trigger words)*.

Remember, whenever you want to settle yourself down and improve your concentration . . . you simply take a deep,

centering breath. . . . Then, on the exhale, say to yourself,
"_____ and _____ . . . ."

Imagine yourself going through that process right now. . . .
Imagine you are about to serve in a match. . . . You can feel
the pressure. . . . You are a little tight in your neck and shoulders. . . . You notice that you are gripping the racket a little
too tightly, . . . and you are worried about getting your serve
in. . . . Feel the pressure. . . . Now, look at the court . . . and
look across the net. . . .

As you look across the net, take that centering breath . . .
and repeat your phrase. . . . At the end of the exhale, notice
that you have soft eyes. . . . You see the whole court. . . . You
feel comfortable. . . . If you like, you may take one more centering breath, and repeat your phrase just before you begin
your ball toss. . . . Then, . . . as you toss the ball, your concentration narrows and you focus on the spot where you are
tossing the ball. . . .

GIVE YOURSELF A MINUTE FOR PRACTICE HERE.

All right, . . . it's time to return to your normal activities. . . .
To do that, count from three to one. . . . On the count of
three, . . . take a deep breath, holding it momentarily. . . .
On the count of two, . . . stretch your arms and legs and exhale. . . . On the count of one, open your eyes and you will be
wide awake, . . . ready to do the things you normally do at
this time. . . . You're feeling good, . . . comfortable, . . . and
relaxed. . . . Ready. . . . Three, . . . take a deep breath. . . . Two, . . .
stretch your arms and legs and exhale. . . . One, . . . open your
eyes, wide awake!

Reprinted, by permission, from R.M. Nideffer, 1992, *Psyched to win*. (Champaign, IL: Human Kinetics), 95-100.

Although you achieve a deeper trance in hetero-hypnosis than in
self-hypnosis, I often teach self-hypnosis so athletes can benefit from
trance phenomenon on their own. Even though the self-induced trance
is lighter, it is deep enough for the athlete to use it for relaxation, reinforcing suggestions, practicing imagery, and facilitating pain relief.

TEACHING SELF-HYPNOSIS

Teaching self-hypnosis requires a deeper trance than I sometimes achieve in the first session, so I usually wait until the second session to do this unless the person has achieved a deep trance in the first session. Before I teach self-hypnosis, I will already have taught the person to enter a trance rapidly when I count from five down to one.

To teach self-hypnosis, I first have the person count with me from five down to one as we reinduce the trance. Then I suggest that the person will be able to self-induce a trance by counting from five down to one. I have the person do this several times in the session to demonstrate the ability to do it. It is usually easy to reenter a trance during the session, because the person will have just come out of a trance. It is not so easy to do it after some time has elapsed, such as when the person is at home or in a different situation. I usually suggest that the person try self-hypnosis several times at home, preferably on the same day as the session in which I taught it.

If at the next session the person reports difficulty in self-induction away from our session, I reinforce these suggestions and practice self-induction in our next session. Going over the procedure a second time usually enables the person to self-induce a trance.

Occasionally, someone will be concerned that the self-hypnosis did not produce as deep a trance as I was able to induce. When this happens, I remind the person that the more times I induced a trance, the deeper the person was able to go, and that with practice they will be able to self-induce a deeper trance.

Many athletes have developed the skills described in the following chapters without hypnosis, but it is clear that a coach or trainer can speed the development of the skills by using the relaxation exercises described later to generate a light trance. Further, some athletes will be able to use a self-induced trance to develop the skills. However, a sport psychologist trained in hypnotherapy, using the techniques described in this book, will enable an athlete to develop these mental skills most rapidly.

BASEBALL'S 90 PERCENT MENTAL, THE OTHER HALF
IS PHYSICAL.

YOGI BERRA, BASEBALL PLAYER

Chapter 2
Taking Mental Training to the Next Level

Most of us remember when our mental state interfered with a good performance. It might have been excessive anxiety in a school exam or meeting a person you wanted to impress. For an athlete, it might occur in an important competition. We know that our mental condition affects how well we perform, but we usually feel that it is not within our control. We would like to control these variations in our mental state that keep us from our optimal functioning.

Neglect of Mental Training

I frequently ask competitive athletes what causes their performances to vary so much—is it differences in their physical condition or in their mental condition? What share of the variation is mental and what is physical? After eliminating temporary health problems and factors out of the athlete's control, most will attribute the differences in performance to the variations in their mental condition. When I ask them to divide the credit between their physical condition and their mental condition, the estimates for the mental share are usually above 50 percent. Yogi's claim that "Baseball's 90 percent mental, the other half is physical" is true of more than baseball.

Although athletes acknowledge that their mental state strongly affects their performance, when I ask them how much training time they spend on the mental aspects of their sport, the estimates are rarely above five percent. Seldom do athletes spend substantial time sharpening their mental skills, and few have any skill or training in this area, yet their mental condition is subject to training as much as their physical conditioning. In general, however, the more skilled the athlete, the greater the understanding of the importance of mental training.

Uses of Mental Training

Mental training covers a variety of skills. The most obvious is the mental state in competition—being able to get into what athletes call the zone. This is the feeling that you are at the peak of your ability, where the actions are smooth and competent and performance is the best. Getting into the zone is often regarded as a chance happening, but skill in controlling both relaxation and arousal—factors important in playing in the zone—is more subject to training than we often realize.

Mental training is not restricted to how you perform in competition, but includes several other areas, such as learning to gain the maximum from practice sessions. Appropriate mental training helps you learn techniques more effectively and develop strength more rapidly. Learning to focus appropriately, to block out the irrelevant, is valuable in both performance and practice. Imagery, learning to practice physical skills mentally, helps develop not only confidence but also the physical skill itself.

Mental training also involves dealing effectively with pain and healing. Considerable evidence exists that an appropriate mental attitude can speed recovery and minimize the frustration of injuries and other performance setbacks. I discuss developing these skills in part II.

Information Gap

The mental training literature is an expanding field. Professional athletes (including Louganis & Marcus, 1995; Montana & Weiner, 1997) as well as sport psychologists and trainers (including Gallwey, 1998; Weinberg & Gould, 1999) have written books and articles. However, few of these publications mention using hypnosis, although it could enhance many techniques the authors pose. Even among athletes who see the importance of mental training, many are not aware or are reluctant to accept that hypnosis can help.

Many books and papers are available on methods of mental training. Rather than review these nonhypnotic methods of mental training, many of which are valuable in developing tough, strong mental attitudes, I will focus on the varied uses of hypnosis that enhance sport performance, often by complementing these other techniques.

Hypnosis and Mental Training

For most sport psychologists, coaches, and athletes, and for this book, using hypnosis for mental training does not include treatment of serious psychological problems. People with serious psychological dysfunctions need the care of a clinical psychologist. Rather, hypnosis can help athletes develop correct techniques and build the concentration, confidence, and willpower essential for maximum performance. The characteristics of hypnosis, such as relaxation, focus, suggestibility, and so on, enable it to make a major impact in developing mental training skills for athletes.

Sport Psychologist's Role

A sport psychologist is trained to develop these mental skills in athletes. Coaches are and have long been adept at developing these skills in their team members, but increasingly sport psychologists are included as members of the training teams. Not all sport psychologists are trained to use the type of hypnotic techniques described in this book, but increasingly hypnotic techniques are included in sport psychology training. Athletes and coaches can use most techniques included here, but often the help of a sport psychologist qualified in hypnotherapy can achieve these goals more effectively.

My Role as a Sport Psychologist

As a sport psychologist it is important not to assume the role of the coach. When I work with an athlete, I am not teaching the physical techniques of a sport. I am concerned only with developing the appropriate mental attitudes and skills to enable the athlete to practice and to perform at his or her best. I feel it is extremely important to work closely with that athlete's coach so the coach understands and has an appropriate input for any work I do with the athlete. Although an important difference exists between the roles of a psychologist and a coach, the two must be complementary to be optimally effective.

When issues come up that the athlete does not want discussed with the coach or others, I accept the athlete's view. Consistent with the ethics of psychotherapy, I regard all conversations with athletes as confidential unless the athlete specifically requests otherwise.

Although I can often help an athlete perfect a technique, the correct technique must be known to the athlete before I begin my work. Often an athlete understands a technique from the coach's description but has not been able to put it into practice. The athlete may have difficulty executing the correct technique because of a prior ingrained habit or some mental block. Sometimes it is caused by the complexity or timing of the action. Generally, with a susceptible and cooperative athlete, hypnosis can help overcome these problems.

Similarly, the sport psychologist's work is not sports medicine. When working with an athlete on pain control or healing, it is important to work closely with the athletic trainer or physician who has organized the athlete's rehabilitation program.

Many recognize that developing a sound mental training program facilitates athletic performance. They know that mental training allows athletes to improve in a variety of ways—in technique, arousal control, motivation, and many other mental aspects of athletics. Now, it is time for athletes, coaches, and sport psychologists to take mental training to the next level using hypnosis.

PART II

DEVELOPING SPECIFIC MENTAL TRAINING SKILLS

Mental training includes the development of a variety of skills. Included are the skills necessary to gain the most from practices, to perform at one's peak in competition, and to recover rapidly from injuries. Achieving these skills is too often left to chance. However, with proper training they will be more likely to fully develop. Part II describes this variety of skills, the nature of each skill, its value to the athlete, and how hypnosis can help facilitate achieving the skill.

YOU MUST RELAX

JACOBSON'S 1976 BOOK TITLE

CHAPTER 3
EASING OUT TENSION

The value of relieving the mental and physical tension of athletes and promoting relaxation is widely recognized. Relaxation and stress reduction are keys not only to top athletic performance, but also to good health and well-being. Gallwey (1998, p. 19) recognizes this when he says, "Relaxed concentration is the key to excellence in all things."

Jacobson's Relaxation Exercise

Jacobson (1929, 1938, 1976) wants people to develop a muscle sense—to know what tension feels like and to recognize and effect an absence of tension. To Jacobson, learning relaxation is learning to recognize and eliminate any feeling of tension. His technique for achieving relaxation requires tensing and relaxing small muscle groups in a prescribed order. In the left leg, for example, he would have the athlete tense and relax in turn the foot flexors, the foot extensors, the leg flexors, the leg extensors, and so on. Most coaches who use a relaxation exercise adapted from Jacobson would have the athlete tense and relax the whole left leg at once. The most familiar technique for inducing relaxation is an exercise such as the following.

RELAXING ATHLETES

The team members lie in comfortable positions on the floor. Then they slowly tense and relax the left leg, the right leg, the right arm, the left arm, the chest, the abdomen, the back, the face, and so on. This continues until they have tensed and relaxed all parts of the body. Ask the athletes to be aware what tenseness feels like and to eliminate all tense feeling as the relaxation takes place. It is also useful to have the athletes exhale as each part of the body relaxes.

Once the athletes are relaxed, the coach can suggest achieving appropriate goals, team spirit, and self-confidence, or ask them to imagine successes in difficult plays or moves.

Several different orders of muscle group tensing have been proposed, but I have not found that the order of the tensing is important, nor does it seem to matter if all body parts get tensed and relaxed. Most athletes can get relaxed after tensing only a few muscle groups. The effect of tensing and relaxing even a few groups decreases tension in the whole body. Clearly though, the more parts of the body tensed and relaxed, the greater the total relaxation.

Light Trance

The tense-and-relax scripts for these relaxation exercises are similar to the progressive relaxation scripts used to induce hypnosis. For athletes particularly susceptible to hypnosis, the result of the relaxation exercises might be a light hypnotic trance, but for others it will be only a relaxed body and mind. I am confident that much of the power of the suggestions made as part of these relaxation exercises is attributable to a light hypnotic trance. When coaches who use this technique are appropriately trained in hypnotic techniques, they will be better able to recognize the possibility and potential of these relaxation exercises.

Suinn's Visual Motor Behavior Rehearsal

Suinn (1976) has formalized Jacobson's relaxation procedure and has termed it Visual Motor Behavior Rehearsal (VMBR). In the VMBR paradigm, the athlete undergoes a carefully prescribed progressive relaxation procedure that is a shortened version of Jacobson's (1976) procedure. Suinn's relaxation procedure takes about 20 minutes for the first session, but after three or four practice sessions, Suinn states that many people can achieve later relaxations in 5 minutes or less. After the athlete is relaxed, the Behavior Rehearsal phase begins. In this phase, the coach makes suggestions about tension or anxiety reduction, team spirit, or goals, and the athlete can image aspects of performance that need attention. Suinn recommends that athletes do the VMBR every day, but at least five days out of seven.

MUSCLE RELAXATION EXERCISE

Muscle relaxation is sought by coaches and athletes because coordination and sustained performance are hindered by muscle tenseness. Relaxation is desirable in nonphysical activities (e.g., mental concentration) because it aids in avoiding distractions to such effort; thus the technique has been used by executives as well.

The directions in the next section are used in a relaxation exercise. As with all physical exercises, the end product is the control by the athlete of muscle groups. In this case the end product is the ability to relax completely within a short time span. With three or four practice sessions, many persons are able to achieve muscle relaxation within five minutes. At this point the muscle tension component of the directions can be omitted.

Relaxation Directions

The primary purpose of the procedure is to aid in focusing attention on how it feels to have muscles truly tense and, in contrast, how it feels to be relaxed (or not tense). In each step you will be asked first to tense a muscle group, then to relax. Always pay close attention to the feeling within the muscles. Tense each muscle group only as long as is required for you to attend to the tension generated. For most, this takes about five seconds or a count of five. Relaxation of the muscle groups takes about the same amount of time. These times are approximate—do not distract yourself by paying too much attention to counting or timing. Tense the muscles until you can really feel the tension, and then relax.

The exercise follows a systematic pattern: right hand (or dominant hand), left hand, right biceps, left biceps, forehead, eyes, facial area, chest, abdomen, legs, and feet. At the start, repeat the exercise for each group twice before going to the next group. Later, omit the tension and the repetition. After completing each muscle group, permit the area to remain relaxed by not moving that area. As a start, someone should read the directions to you.

Hands. First get into a comfortable position, preferably lying down on your back. You may use a small pillow for your head. Choose a time of day when you will not be disturbed for an hour. Many practice in the evening just before falling asleep. The relaxation achieved is an especially good way of going to sleep at night.

Close your eyes so as not to be distracted by your surroundings. Now, tense your right hand into a fist . . . as tight as you can get it . . . so that you can feel the tension . . . really tight, the tighter the better, so that you can really feel the tension. . . . Now relax the hand, let the tension remove itself,. . . feel the muscles become loose,. . . and notice the contrast between the tension a moment ago and the relaxation, the absence of tension. . . . Allow the fingers to relax . . . and then the entire right hand.

Repeat the exercise for the right hand once.

Now we'll leave the right hand relaxed and focus on the left hand. Tense the left hand by making it into a fist . . . very tight . . . and again notice how that tension feels. . . . Focus your attention on the muscles as they are tense. All right, now relax the hand, and notice the contrast between the tension of a moment ago and the relaxation. . . . Continue to be aware of the relaxation of the muscles . . . in the fingers . . . and throughout the entire hand.

Repeat the exercise for the left hand once.

Arms (Biceps). We'll leave the hands and the fingers relaxed and move to the biceps. In order to tense the biceps, you will be bending the arm at the elbow and tightening the biceps by moving your hand toward your shoulder. Let's start with the right arm.

Bend your right arm at the elbow so that your hand moves toward your shoulder . . . tight. . . . Keep tightening the biceps as hard as you can . . . focusing your attention on the muscle tension. . . . Really notice how that feels. . . . Now relax . . . letting the arm and hand drop back down . . . and noticing the relaxation, the absence of tension. . . . Feel the relaxation as it takes over the upper arm. . . . Notice the feeling of relaxation in the lower arm, the hand, and the fingers.

Repeat the exercise for the right arm once.

Now leave the right arm relaxed and move to the left arm. Tense up the left arm by bending it at the elbow . . . really tense, as tense as you can get it . . . and focus your attention on the feelings of tension. . . . Now relax, letting your arm drop back down. . . . Notice the difference in feeling between the tension and the relaxation. . . . Permit the relaxation to take over the entire left arm . . . the upper arm . . . the forearm . . . the hands . . . and fingers.

Repeat the exercise for the left arm once.

Forehead. We'll leave the hands and arms comfortably relaxed and move to the forehead. In order to tense up the forehead, you will frown.

All right, I want you to tense the forehead by frowning. . . . Wrinkle up the forehead area . . . very tight . . . and notice how the tension feels. . . . Now relax. . . . Let the wrinkles smooth themselves out. . . . Allow the relaxation to proceed on its own . . . making the forehead smooth and tension-free, as though you were passing your hand over a sheet to smooth it out.

Repeat the exercise for the forehead once.

Eyes. We'll leave the forehead relaxed and move to the eyes. What I want you to do is close your eyes tighter than they are . . . tighter . . . feeling the tension. . . . (Use less time for the tension here so as to avoid after-images.) Now relax . . . keeping the eyes comfortably closed . . . noticing the contrast between the tension and relaxation now.

Repeat the exercise for the eyes once.

Facial Area. We'll leave the eyes relaxed and go on to the facial area. To tense up the facial area, I want you to clench your jaw. . . . Bite down on your teeth hard now. . . . Really pay attention to the tension in the facial area and jaws. . . . (Use less time for tension here.) Now relax. . . . Let the muscles of the jaw become relaxed. . . . Notice the feeling of relaxation across the lips, the jaw, the entire facial area. . . . Just allow the relaxation to take over.

Repeat the exercise for the facial area once.

All right, notice the relaxation in the right hand and the fingers . . . and the feeling of relaxation in the forearm and the upper arms. . . . Notice the relaxation that is present in the left hand and the fingers . . . in the forearm and the upper arm. . . . Let the relaxation take over and include the forehead . . . smooth and without tension . . . the eyes . . . the facial area . . . and the lips and the jaw.

Chest. All right, we'll now proceed to help relaxation across the chest. I want you to tense up the chest muscles by taking a deep breath and holding it for a moment. . . . Notice the tension. . . . Now slowly exhale, breathing normally again . . . and notice the chest muscles as they become more and more relaxed.

Repeat the exercise for the chest once.

Abdomen. Now we'll move to the abdomen. I want you to tense your abdomen right now . . . very tight. . . . Pay attention to the tension. . . . Now relax . . . letting the feeling of relaxation take over. . . . Notice the difference in the feeling of tension a moment before and the relaxation.

Repeat the exercise for the abdomen once.

Legs and Feet. Now we'll proceed with the relaxation. To tense your legs and feet, I want you to point your toes downward until you can feel the muscles of your legs tense. . . .

Notice the tension. . . . (Use tension for about three seconds, avoid cramping of the toes or feet.) Now relax. . . . Let the relaxation take over. . . . Feel the comfort.

Repeat the exercise for the legs and feet once.

All right, simply enjoy the sense of relaxation and comfort across your body . . . feeling loose and relaxed in the hands and fingers . . . comfortable in the forearms and upper arms . . . noticing the relaxed feeling as it includes the forehead . . . the eyes . . . the facial area . . . the lips and the jaws . . . letting the relaxation include the chest . . . the abdomen . . . and both legs and both feet.

Now, to further increase the relaxation, I want you to take a deep breath and slowly exhale . . . using your rhythmical deep breathing to deepen the relaxation and to permit you to become as relaxed as you want . . . breathing slowly in and out . . . using your rhythm to achieve whatever level of relaxation you want . . . and in the future you can use this deep breathing technique to initiate or to deepen the relaxation whenever you want.

All right, that's fine. . . . Now let your breathing continue normally.

Termination of Exercise. In a moment, I'll count backward from three to one. When I get to one, you'll feel alert and refreshed . . . no aches or pains. . . . You can retain the relaxed feeling as long as you wish. . . . All right, three . . . more and more alert . . . two . . . no aches or pains . . . and one . . . you can open your eyes.

General Instructions

1. If the relaxation exercise is being used for the first time, I recommend that someone reads the instructions aloud for another to follow.

2. Whoever reads the instructions should do so in a normal voice, pacing the speed by doing the tension exercises. The aim is to tense the muscle group long enough to be noticeable but not long enough to be painful, to lead to cramps, or to lead to fatigue.

3. Some muscle groups (e.g., the eyes, the jaws, and the feet) should be tensed for a shorter span, about three seconds, to avoid painful or cramping results.

4. Once an athlete has used the exercise once upon the direction of someone else (as indicated previously), he or she can practice the exercise alone by simply tensing and relaxing each muscle group in sequence.

5. After three or four practice sessions, one can omit the tension part and concentrate on simply having each muscle group become relaxed or limp, again in sequence. With training, a person can develop the relaxation within five minutes; with more practice, individuals have been able to initiate relaxation control within one minute. Such individuals are able to use the relaxation sitting in chairs or riding in vehicles and can practice it prior to contests. Control in relaxing specific muscle groups is possible with repetition.

6. Repetition of the deep breath technique can be a useful signal for initiation of relaxation on a quick reflex basis.

7. Although the relaxation exercise can be used for other forms of training, the directions here are aimed at teaching an individual how to control muscle groups to achieve relaxation. As with any other physical exercise, the success of the exercise requires practice and adherence to the exercise steps. Once a day, five out of every seven days, is a normal routine. More frequent use, such as once daily, speeds up training.

8. For those who wish to speed up the training and who are at training camps with USSA Nordic coaching staff, tape recordings can be made available upon prior arrangement. Contact your coach.

This set of directions was developed by Richard M. Suinn, PhD, Sports Medicine Team, for use by Nordic coaching staff and athletes. Reprinted, by permission, from Dr. Suinn, Professor and Head, Dept. of Psychology, Colorado State University, Fort Collins, Colorado 80523.

Suinn (1976) cites the effective use of VMBR with cross-country and downhill skiers, biathlon competitors, and pistol shooters. Although he says, "the use of VMBR does not seem to demand special skills, such as required, for instance, in the use of imagery through hypnosis," (Suinn, 1993, p. 499), Suinn's relaxation procedure, as with Jacobson's, is likely to generate at least a mild trance in many subjects, which probably explains part of its effectiveness. The relaxed state, even for those not in a trance, allows suggestions to be effective.

Benson's Relaxation Response

Because of the fundamental unity of the mind and the body, it is impossible for one aspect to be relaxed while the other is tense. Jacobson's and Suinn's relaxation techniques aim to produce a relaxed body that will in turn produce a relaxed mind. Herbert Benson (1975, 1987, 1996) is a physician who starts by relaxing the mind, and thus the body. Benson's main concern is with health, rather than with sport performance. He uses a three-legged stool as a metaphor for appropriate treatment of illnesses. One leg of this stool is pharmaceuticals, another leg is procedures such as surgery, and the third leg—the one we are concerned with here—is the patient's self-care. An important part of this self-care is relaxation. Benson has developed techniques that first relax the mind, then relax the body. Benson's original interest was relaxation in the service of healing and his findings established that relaxation exercises, practiced regularly, are effective in promoting good health.

> In my 30 years of practicing medicine, I've found no healing force more impressive or more universally available than the power of the individual to care for and cure him- or herself.
>
> Herbert Benson, cardiologist, Harvard Medical School

Benson's Foundation

Benson has based his techniques on those of Transcendental Meditation (TM). TM first gained popularity in the United States in the 1960s and soon became America's most popular form of meditation with probably several million adherents. Benson worked with Maharishi Mahesh Yogi, the developer and main proponent of TM in the United States, to develop his Relaxation Response—basically a simplified form of TM. Benson attempted to find the essential elements of TM's relaxation and eliminate the mumbo jumbo that often surrounds TM. Because the purpose of any relaxation exercise is to relax both the body and the mind, it is optional whether you go from the mind to the body or the body to the mind. Benson's techniques are described in detail in several of his books.

Benson's Procedure

Benson's procedure for eliciting the relaxation response includes seven steps.

1. Pick a focus word that has a significant meaning for you.
2. Sit in a comfortable position with a relaxed posture.
3. Close the eyes.
4. Relax the muscles.
5. Breathe smoothly and naturally, repeating the focus word selected in step 1 with each exhale.
6. Be passive. If other thoughts come, dismiss them with, "Oh well," and calmly return to the focus word. Don't worry about how the process is going.
7. Continue this for 10 to 20 minutes.

After this procedure, Benson's Relaxation Response (RR) is established. Benson claims that this RR makes the right brain more accessible to suggestions—as we noted earlier, a characteristic also of hypnosis. Just as after the relaxation phase of Suinn's VMBR, when the RR is achieved, all imagery and suggestions are more powerful in their effect.

Like Suinn, Benson recommends that individuals do a RR frequently. Benson has found substantial health benefits come from establishing the RR once or twice a day —making it a permanent part of one's daily routine.

Benson's main interest is general health, but he also suggests sports applications of his Relaxation Response in *Your Maximum Mind* (1987). Although not yet as widely used as muscular relaxation techniques, the Relaxation Response is occasionally referred to in sports literature. Whitmark (1998), for example, recommends it for relaxing bodybuilders.

Hypnotic Relaxation

Although Jacobson, Suinn, and Benson have developed effective techniques for reaching a relaxed state, hypnosis can bring about this relaxation more rapidly than any of these procedures. An initial heterohypnotic induction usually takes less than five minutes, and a reinduction may take only 5 to 10 seconds. If I sense that the person is not deep, elements of either Suinn's or Benson's technique can deepen the participant's trance and relax the participant further. When using Suinn, I ask the athlete to slowly tense and relax one or several groups of muscles. If an athlete is in even a light trance, tensing and relaxing only one or two muscle groups will generate more relaxation. When using Benson, I ask the athlete to say, "Relax," with each exhale and to feel the whole mind and body becoming relaxed. Either approach effectively deepens a trance and the athlete's relaxation.

REINDUCTION

I have found that it saves time to teach each person I work with to enter a trance rapidly. Although an initial induction does not take long—from two minutes to five minutes—it is convenient to induce a trance even more rapidly, so I routinely teach a rapid reinduction procedure. This is useful if I work with the person a second time, but also convenient in the first session when I want to bring a person in and out of a trance several times. Multiple reinductions (termed fractionation) produce deeper and deeper trances, and that is often part of my procedure.

While individuals are in a trance, I suggest that I will later ask them if they are willing to be rehypnotized. If they are willing, they can indicate this by nodding or saying, "Yes." I tell them I will count down from five to one (each number at about one-second intervals). As I count down, I suggest that the person will feel a relaxation in the body. At about three, the eyes will be so relaxed that they will close, and at one, the whole body will be nicely relaxed and in a trance.

Also while in a trance, I tell each person that I will be able to terminate the trance by counting slowly from one up to five. At three or four the eyes will open, and at five the person will be completely awake and alert. Because occasionally someone worries about being stuck in a trance, I also tell them they will be able to come out of the trance at any time they want by counting slowly from one up to five. I have them practice each procedure, that is, entering and coming out of a trance, several times so they feel comfortable with a rapid reinduction as well as with bringing themselves out of a trance.

The efficiency of hypnosis in relaxing an athlete is substantial. Even if some deepening is needed, this can be effected in less than a minute. During the initial trance, an athlete can be given a posthypnotic suggestion that will enable a later reinduction and relaxation in five seconds or less. Likewise, with self-hypnosis, the athlete can independently enter a trance and gain this relaxation in the same short time.

Value of Hypnotic Relaxation

The relaxed state facilitates most other uses of hypnosis, such as imagery, ego-enhancement, goal setting, pain alleviation, and controlling performance arousal and focus. When the body and the mind are both relaxed, the athlete is more able to image a perfect performance, to accept suggestions, to set appropriate goals, and to learn to effect ideal levels of arousal. These uses of relaxation are covered in more detail in later chapters.

In addition to suggestions that can be made to an athlete in a relaxed state, the relaxation itself is valuable—Benson stresses its value to general health. Likewise, hypnosis can be an effective supplement to stretching exercises. Athletes who learn to do their stretching in a light trance find they achieve flexibility rapidly and thoroughly.

An athlete in a relaxed and flexible state can perform more smoothly and is much less susceptible to injuries. However, the term relaxed, when applied to how an athlete should feel when participating in a sport, may be misleading. The desired relaxation is not the flaccid state produced by Suinn's VMBR, Benson's RR, or the relaxation associated with a trance. Rather, the relaxed athlete feels a power and control unhampered by any debilitating tension and functions with a smoothness and fluidity of motion. Some athletes describe this as a feeling of flow (Csikszentmihalyi, 1990). Hypnosis and imagery can help an athlete achieve this performance state.

Excessive Relaxation

Relaxing an athlete for competition is not always the appropriate procedure. Athletes need a certain degree of tension or energy level to perform well. The appropriate amount of tension is unique to each athlete—it varies from sport to sport and from athlete to athlete.

BEING TOO RELAXED

A boxer who was concerned about his excess tension before and during a match learned to relax at the start of the match. The relaxation made him enjoy the match, until his relaxed state caused him to lose his fighting edge—and the match.

Controlling Relaxation

Control of your relaxation level is an important skill. As suggested with the boxer, a low level of tension is not always an appropriate goal—neither is a high level. Arriving at the optimum level is not a difficult task, because athletes in a trance can image themselves at their optimum arousal level, and this is the level I help them achieve. Chapter 7, "Optimizing Arousal Levels," describes techniques for assuring the optimum arousal level.

RELAXING A FOOTBALL PLAYER

It is possible in hypnosis to teach an athlete to control his relaxation. A football player, let's call him Greg, was finding himself too tense in games. The coach had asked me to see if I could help Greg be less tense during the games. It appeared that Greg psyched himself up before a game and stayed at this high level of tension all through the game. He was afraid that if he relaxed at any time during the game, he would lose his competitive edge. In the latter part of any game, when the coach needed him at his full power, he found himself too tired to perform well. When I watched him during a game, he always seemed to be at a high pitch, even when he was on the sidelines watching the offensive team.

I worked with Greg in an individual session. We started by estimating how many minutes in a football game he had to be at his peak. Because he was on the sidelines about half the time while the offense was playing, and there was time between plays, we calculated that he needed to be at a peak for only 5 to 10 minutes in a full game. If Greg could relax during many of the 50 minutes he was not playing, he would be better able to sustain his high level of arousal during those

10 minutes when he needed to be up. He was concerned that if he relaxed during the time he was not involved in a play, he would not be able to get back to an effective level of arousal when he needed to be up and involved.

I used a progressive relaxation induction and found Greg susceptible to hypnosis. In general, athletes who have identified a problem and feel that hypnosis will help them with that problem are susceptible to a trance. Because I would be working with relaxation, I used parts of Suinn's tense-and-relax script (see page 27) to achieve more relaxation and to deepen Greg's trance.

While in a trance, we first worked on a signal he could initiate to get up to his effective alert status. Greg's main concern was that he be at a good peak of energy whenever he needed to be, so we first worked on a way to get to that arousal level. I first had him see himself in a game and at the optimum level of arousal for him. I asked him to describe how his body felt and how his mind felt. He was able to see his body as strong, fast, and bursting with energy and his mind as clear, focused, and confident. I grasped his elbow and said that this touch would remind him of these feelings. Then I had him relax again. I told him that the signal for him to reestablish this condition was a couple deep breaths using his abdominal muscles and saying, "Focus," with each breath. I had him image doing this without a reference to being in a game. I then had him see himself in a game situation achieving his arousal. We repeated this several times until he found he could reestablish an appropriate arousal quickly. All this was accomplished while Greg was in a trance.

When he felt he was able to achieve this energy level at will, we began to work on a signal to relax. We used the referee's whistle as the signal to relax. Only because he knew he could reestablish his arousal was he able to feel that he could safely relax when the referee's whistle signaled the end of a play. We imaged using these signals to relax, then regain his arousal edge a number of times, until he felt comfortable shifting from one mode to the other and was sure he could do it. The imaging at first was shifting back and forth from a relaxed mode to an up-for-action mode while in our session, but soon he was imaging a game situation and using the signals to shift from one mode to the other.

He used the signals in the next game and was astounded at how quickly and easily he could get from one mode to the other. At one point, when the offense was playing, he relaxed enough to sit on the bench. Although that doesn't sound like much, it was a major change for him. He had never understood how a player could sit down and relax during a game.

He found that maintaining such a high level of tension was not necessary in his performance, and he even felt that when he was not so tense he played more effectively, particularly in the latter parts of the game. When I talked to him at the end of the game, he was astounded and delighted that he felt as fresh as he had at the start and could have played another game right then. I laughed (sympathetically of course) and asked him why someone in his good physical condition would be exhausted at the end of only 5 to 10 minutes of activity. He smiled and understood. The coach, who had asked me to help him with the problem, was delighted at his capability at the end of the game.

Relaxation and Pain

Relaxation can be useful with certain types of pain. Pain and tension are frequently associated. When a muscle is in pain from an injury, the body tends to tighten that muscle. This in turn increases the pain, which further increases the tension in that muscle. Back pains frequently have this cycle of pain and tension. Hypnosis can both induce relaxation and reduce pain, thus effectively breaking the pain-tension cycle. When you can ease and relax injured muscles, the pain subsides. As the pain subsides, the muscles can relax more, breaking the pain-tension cycle and relieving the pain. Also, a relaxed muscle can heal itself more rapidly than a muscle under tension.

The ability to control your relaxation is valuable in many ways. The relaxation techniques of Suinn and Benson allow the mind and body to respond to suggestions for improvement. Being able to relax at appropriate times in a competition allows an athlete to conserve energy for when it is needed. Further, relaxation is fundamental to many mental skills described in other chapters of this book and is closely related to arousal control. Relaxation is an important mental skill and the key to unlocking many other basic mental skills of athletes.

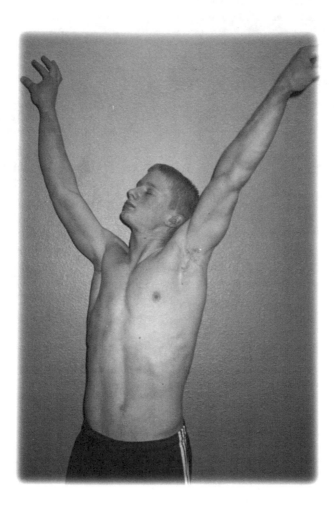

SEE YOUR FUTURE, BE YOUR FUTURE.

JOE NAMATH, FOOTBALL QUARTERBACK

Chapter 4
Imaging Perfect Performance

In the literature, the terms imagery and visualization have been used interchangeably. I prefer to use the term imagery rather than visualization, because visualization implies only seeing, and seeing is just one aspect of the phenomenon of imagery. Other aspects, particularly the kinesthetic and the emotional, are as important as the visual for the effectiveness of imagery.

Value of Imagery

Many sport psychologists, elite athletes, and all standard sport psychology texts encourage the use of imagery. Gould and Damarjian's (1996, p. 26) statement is typical:

> To begin with, it should be made clear that we believe in the power of imagery and its importance as a psychological skill for enhancing athletic performance. As we convey in this chapter, research has clearly demonstrated the efficacy of imagery as a sport psychological change mechanism.

Imagery is helpful in controlling anxiety (or arousal); facilitating relaxation; improving self-confidence and motivation; and facilitating performance, often in a nonspecific way.

DEMONSTRATING THE POWER OF IMAGERY

It is possible to demonstrate the power of imagery simply. Ask a person to make a circle with the thumb and forefinger (see figure 4.1a), and to hold this ring tightly while a second

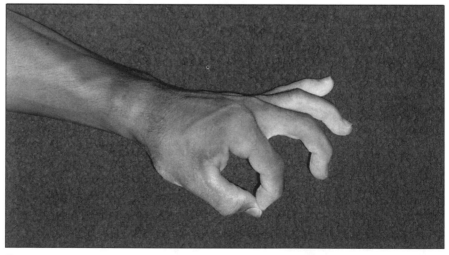

a

Figure 4.1 *(a)* Forming a ring with the thumb and forefinger.

(continued)

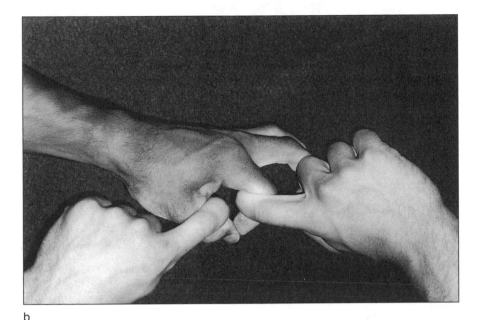

b

Figure 4.1 *(continued)*   *(b)* Pulling the fingers apart.

person tries to pull apart the thumb and the forefinger (see figure 4.1b). Unless the first person is much stronger than the second, the second person will be able to pull the thumb from the forefinger. Then ask the first person to imagine a strong steel ring in the circle made by the thumb and the forefinger and that this ring is holding the thumb to the finger. When the first person has imaged this, the second person can attempt again to pull the finger and thumb apart. The solidity of the ring will have dramatically changed the strength of the fingers. This demonstration does not require a trance state.

Experiencing Imagery

Many athletes have recognized the value of imagery in practicing or solidifying a technique. Suinn (1993) cites statements from a variety of athletes who depend on imagery to enhance their performance—skier Jean-Claude Killy, golfer Jack Nicklaus, tennis pro Chris Evert, high jumper Dwight Stones, and defensive end Bill Glass.

LEARNING A NEW DIVE

Greg Louganis (Louganis & Marcus, 1995) described how he used imagery when learning a dive. He would visualize someone doing the dive in slow motion, taking about three seconds for the dive. He would then take the dive apart and see each element as the dive slowly progressed. Then he would feel himself doing the dive in slow motion, gradually increasing the speed of the dive as he became familiar with it.

Research on Imagery

A substantial body of research supports athletes' reliance on imagery. Martin and Hall (1995) experimentally tested the effects of imagery on 39 beginning golfers. Those using imagery set higher goals, had more realistic self-expectations, spent more time practicing, and adhered more to their training program. Highlen and Bennett (1983) compared the use of imagery by less successful and more successful elite divers and wrestlers: the more successful athletes used more imagery in both practice and competition, and they experienced more vivid and clear imagery.

In addition to noting the familiar use of imagery in developing and practicing motor skills and strategies, Martens (1982) lists several other uses for imagery—setting goals and motivating achievement, learning to control emotions, focusing or concentrating energy and attention, and increasing self-confidence and self-awareness. In the appendix to his article, he tabulates the results of 31 studies in which imagery was used to enhance athletic performance.

Although some evidence exists that imagery helps the cognitive aspects of the sport more than it helps the motor aspects (Ryan & Simons, 1983), both cognitive and motor aspects are crucial in most sports, and the potential of imagery is widely applicable.

Feltz and Landers (1983) performed a meta-analysis on 60 studies assessing the effects of imagery on performance. Although they found some studies in which imagery had no effect, and occasionally a negative effect, on performance, overall the studies supported the use of imagery. The effect was least significant on strict strength tests (M = 0.20), larger for motor tasks (M = 0.43), and largest for performances with a cognitive component (M = 1.44). The effect was positive for both early and later stages of learning.

Research since the Feltz and Landers (1983) study has continued to support imagery, although an occasional study finds it has a negative effect. For example, Tenenbaum, Bar-Eli, Hoffman, and Jablonovski (1995) found a small negative effect of imagery on a strength performance, the performance Feltz and Landers found least susceptible to imagery enhancement.

Appropriate Imagery

When doing imagery, it is important that the image be of the performance you want to achieve, because the image is a powerful control of future performance. Although imaging success will not always produce success, imaging yourself in doubt or failure is likely to interfere with good performance.

CONTROLLING IMAGES

When I asked a pool player whether he used imagery, he assured me that he had long used imagery. He had found it valuable in letting him know whether he could make a shot or not. Before each shot he would image the result, and he could tell from the imagery whether he would be successful or not. He said that if the image was successful, he knew he would make the shot, but if the image was a missed shot, he knew the shot would be bad.

He viewed the imagery as a prediction, not as a control. I suggested that any time he imaged a missed shot he should image the shot again and to continue reimaging that shot until he achieved a successful image. I wanted him to see his imagery as a way of controlling his shot, rather than seeing the image as a forecast of success or failure. A considerable portion of his income came from shooting pool, and this ability to predict success was valuable to him in his game. He called me a few days after our session to say that the next night after our session he had reimaged each of his missed-shot images until he could see himself successful. By getting a successful image for each shot, he had won back more than the cost of our session in that one night. It made me wonder if I should start charging my clients on a commission basis!

Another athlete found a different advantage from imaging success. After experiencing several perfect images, she felt as though she had already accomplished the performance, and this gave her the confidence that it was inevitable that she would do it perfectly again.

Hypnosis and Imagery

Although imagery has long been a part of the training routines of athletes, the contribution of hypnosis in enhancing the intensity of imaging is far less recognized. Hypnosis seems to stand on the fringe of respectability, with its potential for enhancing imagery rarely recognized or realized.

Enhancing Imagery Through a Trance

Though people often do imagery without a trance, imagery in a trance is significantly more vivid and powerful. In a recent study (Liggett, 2000), I asked the participants to image a variety of situations—practicing their sport alone, practicing in front of others, watching a teammate make a mistake, and competing in a meet. The participants imaged each situation in and out of a trance—half the time the hypnotic imagery was first and the rest of the time the hypnotic imagery was second. I asked them to use a five-point scale to assess the subjective vividness of the imagery on four dimensions.

1. How vividly did they see?
2. How vividly did they hear?
3. How much did they feel kinesthetically?
4. How much emotion did they sense?

The athletes included gymnasts; golfers; mountain bikers; and rugby, tennis, water polo, and soccer players. The increased vividness of hypnotic imagery was significant whether the hypnotic imagery came first or second, whatever sport they imaged, and whatever aspect of imagery they measured. Figure 4.2 summarizes the results of the study.

Clearly hypnosis enhanced the vividness of imagery. The study did not assess whether more vivid imagery results in more effective imagery, but logic and my experience suggest that this is true.

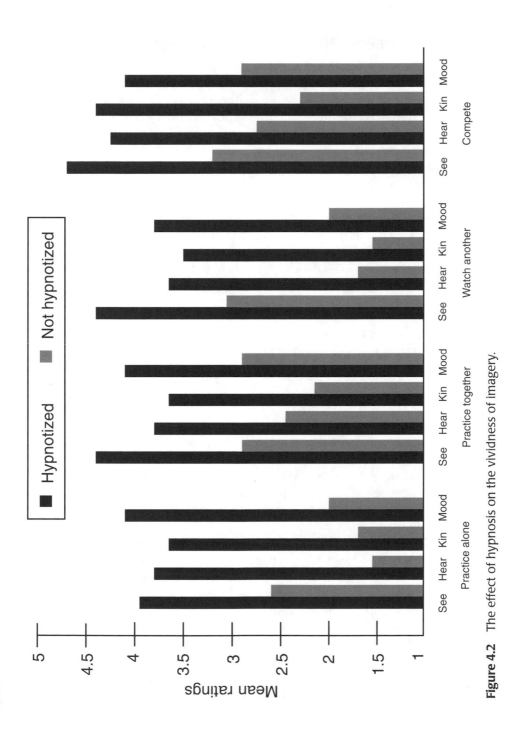

Figure 4.2 The effect of hypnosis on the vividness of imagery.

Slowing Reality Through Trance Imagery

An additional advantage of imagery in a trance is that the subject can slow reality. An ability to distort perceptions, in this case time, is one characteristic of a trance. This time distortion has been effective in perfecting actions that the athlete cannot rehearse slowly. Although a shot-putter can go through her steps slowly to perfect them, a diver can rehearse a complex dive slowly only through imagery. Slow-motion internal imagery in a trance is an effective way to develop this type of technique. As described earlier, Greg Louganis (Louganis & Marcus, 1995) effectively used slow-motion imagery to learn a new dive, but the imagery might have been more effective if he had done it in a trance.

In the cases that follow, the individuals accomplished the imagery in a trance. Although nontrance imagery can be successful, I have found that trance imagery is so much more vivid that it is usually my modus operandi.

CASE ONE: PERFECTING A DOUBLE BACK FLIP

A gymnast needed help to perfect a double back flip with a full twist—a trick he had been working on for almost two years (Liggett & Hamada, 1993). He knew what the timing should be but was rarely able to get the timing right to stick the flip. He was not confident that hypnosis would help, but he was willing to try. I used a progressive relaxation induction with him. He entered a trance easily, and I did not feel any deepening was necessary (though with progressive relaxation, it is not clear when trance induction ends and deepening begins).

In a trance, I asked him to go over exactly what he needed to do to land the trick precisely. After we did this, I asked him to feel himself doing the trick slowly—slow enough to get the timing exactly right. The gymnast orally described the procedure as he felt himself doing the trick in slow motion. He repeated this several times. As soon as he was able to feel himself getting the timing exactly correct, I asked him if he could image the flip at a slightly greater speed and maintain the correct timing. He was able to repeat the imagery at gradually increasing speeds, always maintaining the correct timing and form, until he could comfortably do the flip at real speed. Then, while still in a trance, he imaged repeating the flip several times at full speed until the correct responses were well anchored. After the session, which took a little less than an hour, he was able to perform the flip five times in a row and later incorporated it into his floor routine.

CASE TWO: EASING A PERFORMANCE BLOCK

I used a slightly different technique with two other gymnasts. Each had experienced a painful injury, one on a dismount and one on a release, and was subsequently unable to perform these moves. For each of them, the debilitating block had lasted more than six months—well past the physical recovery from the injuries. Both wanted to include the tricks in their competition routines, but they could not bring themselves to attempt the tricks, even in practice. Both had tried imagery to overcome their blocks, but they had not tried hypnotic imagery.

I worked with each gymnast individually. Both athletes were almost desperate to regain their ability for the tricks and thus proved susceptible to hypnosis. In a trance, I had each go back to the competition where the injury occurred and to feel themselves in that competition. When they got to the point where they made the mistake that caused the injury, they were to stop the procedure, back up a bit as though they were rewinding a video tape, correct the move, then perform the move successfully. Then I asked them to feel themselves doing the trick successfully several times at that meet and to feel the confidence of the success. After imaging the trick successfully in the venue where the injury occurred, I had each gymnast image doing the trick several times at the home gym, then in a future competition. After they were brought out of the trance, both were able to do the tricks with some comfort.

I talked to them afterward to analyze how the technique worked. Both fully remembered what had transpired in the trance. Each said that before I worked with him he knew intellectually that he should be able to do the trick without injury, but when it came to doing it, a mental block, a fear, stopped him. After the session, intellectually he still knew that the last time he did the trick he was injured but somehow he had a recollection that he had completed the trick successfully several times since the accident. Thus, emotionally he now knew he could do it successfully.

This change in right-brain and left-brain thinking is explainable. The intellectually oriented left brain knew the trick could be done, but the emotionally oriented right brain knew of the injury and focused on the danger. When in conflict, the emotions almost always have more power than the intellect. The successful completions of the trick in a trance had assured the emotionally oriented right brain that it was safe to do the trick again.

Internal and External Imagery

There is no widely agreed upon terminology for different types of imagery, though several types are recognized. Some imagery is merely a mental rehearsal of an act. The imager mentally describes the steps in an act or sees himself or herself as though watching on a TV screen. It is becoming standard to use the term external imagery when there is only this type of mental picture.

In another type, the imager sees what would be seen if a camera were attached to the helmet. In this type, the imager may or may not feel a kinesthetic reaction during the imagery. When an imager feels movement in the muscles, that is, when there is a kinesthetic reaction, imagery is more effective. Weinberg and Gould (1999) use internal imagery when the imager sees what he or she would see in the performance whether or not he or she feels the act kinesthetically. When there is a kinesthetic reaction, an observer can usually see the imager's muscles contract or twitch, sometimes slightly, sometimes vigorously.

Distinguishing Between Internal and Kinesthetic Imagery

Jim Bauman (personal communication), the sport psychologist for the U.S. Olympic Training Center, San Diego, feels it is important to separate imagery into three types. The first is the external imagery described previously. In the second type, the athlete sees what he or she would see were he or she performing the sport, as though there were a camera on the head. The third type is the kinesthetic imagery I call internal imagery. This trichotomy provides a way to describe the nature of imagery.

Power of Kinesthetic Imagery

Kinesthetic imagery is the most powerful type of imagery you can use to perfect a technique. I encourage a kinesthetic reaction when imaging. In one theory explaining the effectiveness of kinesthetic imagery, Bandura (1986, pp. 61-62) found that in kinesthetic imagery the brain sends the signals to the same muscles used in practice. Because the subject is likely to image a perfect performance, imaging an act can often be more valuable than physical practice. Bandura suggests that imagery benefits performance by "creating an appropriate cognitive set for the activity, by diverting attention from stressful disruptive thoughts to more helpful ones, or by boosting perceived self-efficacy." Obviously physical practice is necessary, but using imagery is a valuable supplement to it. In the examples cited earlier in this chapter, I used kinesthetic imagery to achieve the results.

When describing the process of imagery, I prefer to ask an athlete to image a performance, rather than to imagine it. I feel this subtle difference makes the experience and the resulting image more real. I haven't formally tested this hypothesis, but I operate—I image—that it is true.

Identification Imagery

In another type of imagery, the subject identifies with something or someone who holds the attributes the athlete wants to acquire. In this imagery, the athlete may identify with a famous person, an animal, or even an inanimate object or machine with the desired characteristics.

Imaging an Expert

You can use the identification imagery technique to help an athlete copy the form and strength of an expert. This is probably the most familiar type of imagery. Young basketball players become Michael Jordans, boxers become Mike Tysons or Evander Holyfields, and figure skaters become Michele Kwans. This imagery is more than just pretend—it helps an athlete develop. Imaging the expert's form and then merging with the expert allows the athlete to feel the correct form in the relevant muscles of the body. A hypnotic trance is not necessary, but it does enhance the imaging substantially.

Bill Russell (Russell & Branch, 1979, pp. 66-67), a five-time Most Valuable Player of the NBA and a Basketball Hall of Fame selection, described his use of imagery as follows.

> On this particular night I was working on replays of many plays, including McKelvey's way of taking an offensive rebound and moving quickly to the hoop. It's a fairly simple play for any big man in basketball, but I didn't execute it well and McKelvey did. Since I had an accurate version of his technique in my head, I started playing with the image right there on the bench, running back the picture several times and each time inserting part of me for McKelvey. Finally I saw myself making the whole move, and I ran this over and over, too. When I went into the game, I grabbed an offensive rebound and put it in the basket just the way McKelvey did. It seemed natural, almost as if I were just stepping into a film and following the signs. When the imitation worked and the ball went in, I could barely contain myself. I was so elated I thought I would float right out of the gym. Every time I'd tried to copy moves in the past, I'd dribbled the ball off my arm or committed some other goof. Now for the first time I had transferred something from my head to my body. It seemed so easy. My first dose of athletic confidence was coming to me when I was 18 years old.

The tapes made by SyberVision are good examples of the effectiveness of imaging an expert. Each tape shows experts in a sport demonstrating perfect form in that sport. SyberVision tapes have been developed for skiing, golf, tennis, baseball, and other sports (SyberVision, 1996). One part of the skiing tape, for example, shows an expert demonstrating perfect form several times for a specific turn. The observers watch, then feel themselves performing the skill as they watch the tape. The tape shows correct form for various parts of the body as the observers image that turn. For example, the tape first emphasizes what the knees should be doing, and the observer is to watch, then image the correct form for the knees. Then the tape emphasizes hands and arms. After they demonstrate this turn, the experts demonstrate another type of turn. Each time, the observers are asked to experience a kinesthetic reaction (internal imagery) as they watch the tapes.

Although the SyberVision tapes do not mention hypnosis, their effectiveness would probably be increased markedly if the observer were in a self-induced trance.

Imaging an Animal

Although it is often useful to image another athlete, an appropriate image might be an animal that has a characteristic the athlete wishes to achieve. Muhammad Ali's, "Float like a butterfly, sting like a bee," is an example of a relevant animal image.

BEING THE PANTHER

A college football lineman was having trouble with slow times on his 40-yard dash. When I watched him in his 40-yard time trials, he appeared to be awkwardly tense. In games, he appeared smoother, with more free-flowing ease. The tenseness seemed to appear when he was being timed in the 40-yard run. I asked him to think of a fast animal, and he selected a black panther. (Usually when athletes do this, the animal they pick is one of the wild cats—a cheetah, panther, or such.) The athlete, when in a trance, was to observe how the panther combined strength and relaxation when it ran—to observe how the legs tense only for the power stroke, then relax on the return, and how smoothly this makes the cat run. I invited the runner to feel himself running and gradually merge with the panther—to capture this power and relaxation, to merge with the panther and feel himself running smoothly with the cat's combination of power and relaxation. The athlete did this first in slow motion, then gradually sped up. After completing several real-time imagings of the 40-yard dash with this technique, the subject was able to apply the technique in an actual run.

Although his previous timings were all over 5.00 seconds, the next time he ran it in 4.85. This was a chunky lineman, and although 4.85 is not a great time for a 40-yard dash, it was more respectable than the 5.00 plus. He was later able to bring the time down another 0.2 seconds by repeatedly imaging himself as a panther. As with many athletes who learn to relax while performing, he was astounded at how his effort level went down as the speed increased. He had tried to get more speed by more effort and was surprised to find the gain came from less effort.

Other Imaging

Sometimes it is advantageous to have an athlete image something other than a living model—a machine with a characteristic to copy. A long-distance runner was having trouble running out of steam at a certain point in his race. I asked him to imagine a machine that did not get tired. He pictured a steam locomotive, constantly speeding along with no fatigue. While in a trance, he captured the energy of this locomotive by imaging himself as the locomotive and was able to use this image in his race to get past his prior wall.

SPRINGING TO SUCCESS

A pole-vaulter felt trouble getting a strong enough spring on his takeoff. After an induction, I asked him to imagine that he was taking off from a trampoline, rather than from solid ground. He had been a diver and had used a trampoline in that sport, so he was familiar with the lift from a trampoline. I suggested that he image feeling the lift of the trampoline as he took off from the ramp for his vault. We repeated this image several times, and I suggested that he would feel this lift when he vaulted in the field. When later he vaulted, he said he clearly felt the lift from the trampoline. In the next meet he vaulted 15 inches higher than in any previous meet. (We cannot attribute all of this gain to the trampoline. He had been having trouble performing in meets as well as he did in practice, and we had worked on that problem too. I describe this case more fully in chapter 15, "Jim, the Pole-Vaulter.")

I can explain the effectiveness of the thumb-finger exercise and the runner's improvement by the concept of agonist and antagonist muscles. When the subject holds the thumb and forefinger together, he or she will tighten all the muscles of the two digits—the muscles that hold the fingers together and those that would pull them apart. When imaging a ring of steel, the subject seems to use only the agonist muscles—those necessary to hold the integrity of the ring. If the subject applies the same force to open the ring in both situations, he or she will usually feel that much less effort was required when the steel ring is imaged. This seems to be because the subject is activating only the agonist muscles.

Similarly, when the runner was running his first time trials, he tightened many more muscles than he needed to—those that made him run fast and those that did not provide him with any running speed or power. His running looked jerky and awkward. Imaging a relaxed fluidity allowed him to use the full power of his legs. Thus the runner felt himself expending much less effort when he imaged the panther.

Imaging seems to be the most effective way to help an athlete relax the antagonist muscles. Telling a person to relax those muscles is generally met with a perplexed, "How do I do that?" reaction. Because this relaxation is such a significant skill, imaging becomes an important facilitating skill. In my experience, imaging in a trance is considerably more powerful than imaging without hypnosis. The gymnasts with the block, the gymnast learning the double back flip, the distance runner, the pole-vaulter, and the football player had all tried imagery without hypnosis, and all found it was the imagery with hypnosis that allowed them to achieve their goals.

SOME CLAIM WE USE ONLY 10 PERCENT OF OUR BRAIN
CELLS. WHAT IF THIS IS ALSO TRUE FOR OUR MUSCLE
CELLS?

DON LIGGETT

CHAPTER 5
MOBILIZING ENERGY

In some sports, success requires a large and carefully controlled burst of energy. Examples include many combinations of strength and control—a golf drive requires high precision as well as strength; a shot put requires a carefully controlled burst of energy and less directional precision. Hypnosis can aid in bringing all the appropriate muscles into play and in channelling this energy burst.

Technique Is Still Important

The emphasis on controlling energy is not to minimize technique in either golfing or shot putting, but to say that control of the direction of the ball is less important in shot putting than in golf. A baseball player once explained why he played baseball rather than golf by pointing out that a home run was good whether it went over the left field or right field fence, but a golf drive always had to be exactly over second base.

Among other events requiring a burst of energy and good technique are the high jump, pole vault, and weightlifting. Although this chapter is about enhancing that burst of energy, do not underestimate the necessity of good technique in such activities.

Hypnosis Boosts Energy

Hypnosis can help two aspects of this energy burst. The first is to increase the amount of energy in the burst. Second is to incorporate all the relevant muscles in the energy burst.

Releasing the Maximum Energy

To help athletes release the maximum energy, it is useful for them to know their maximum energy is available when exhaling. Thus the burst of energy in a shot put or a high jump should come as the athlete exhales. The same is true for push-ups. Exhale when pushing up, inhale when going down.

GAINING ENERGY

To get the maximum energy, I suggest that the athlete inhale and feel the energy coming in. When this can fit the event, the athlete will exhale after the first deep breath, then inhale again, and perform the act when exhaling the second time. The timing of these two breaths is different for different sports. For a high jump, the athlete may inhale and exhale at the end of the ramp before starting the run, inhale during the run, and exhale with the jump. A shot-putter would inhale, exhale, inhale, and exhale while making the throw. Making these suggestions while an athlete is in a trance strengthens the feeling of power when making the leap or throw.

Using the Entire Body

Although in these events, the effort may appear to focus on only a few muscles, appropriate technique ensures that the entire body contributes to the strength and accuracy of the burst—that the athlete's energy comes from all relevant muscles at once. All the body's muscles, particularly the muscles of the torso, participate in a golf drive as well as in a shot put. To concentrate mainly on the arm muscles in either of these is to miss the full burst of strength and control. The athlete's energy must come from the complete set of relevant muscles at once. Often, the coach describes the correct technique but does not guide the athlete to feel the technique's effect on the muscles involved. Athletes can facilitate this release of energy by using internal imagery under hypnosis.

MAKING THE LONG DRIVES

The example of golf is relevant here. Tiger Woods is not a large, muscular person, but his long drives are the envy of many professionals. The only way he can produce this distance in his drive is to bring completely into play his body's entire force—his arms, torso, and legs. In a good golf stroke, the body acts like a coiled spring. All parts of this spring, from the soles of the shoes to the end of the upraised club, must contribute to the power of the stroke. The many form recommendations in golf—keep your arm stiff, keep weight even on both feet, shift your weight as the club comes down, follow through, keep elbow at a right angle, and so on—are designed to bring into coordinated force all the golfer's muscles from the toes to the wrists and fingers. Focusing on the way the form change involves additional muscles and not just on the form change helps to activate those appropriate muscles. The vivid imagery possible in hypnosis can enhance this form change.

Team Effort

The possibility of increased power when you bring more muscles into the task is common to many sports. It is not the sport psychologist's function to know or teach the appropriate techniques for improving the athlete's performance. It is impossible for a psychologist to know the proper technique for all the sports in which he or she might be involved. Technique is a coach's function. To help an athlete improve the technique, the athlete must know the proper technique and must understand what to do. Therefore, the sport psychologist using hypnosis needs to work closely with a competent coach to be sure the athlete understands what is desired. Then, the sport psychologist can help the athlete image, and thus practice, a correct technique and better understand the effect of the correct technique. I explain the techniques of imagery more fully in chapter 4, "Imaging Perfect Performance."

WORKING TOGETHER

My usual method is to work with the coach and the athlete to determine weak aspects of the technique. My sessions with the athlete will concentrate on these aspects. Usually the recommendation is to change the position of some body part. The real problem is usually that some part of the body is not making the appropriate contribution to the exertion. It might be some part is overexercising or that some other part is not contributing to the throw. If the technique suggestion comes from the coach, I make sure the athlete clearly understands what to do. Although correcting the technique may not seem to bring additional muscles into the activity, this is often the purpose, and it usually helps for the athlete to feel the increased contribution of that muscle or muscle group.

Hypnosis is helpful when an athlete is changing a technique. The athlete needs to understand the new technique and what muscles will be affected by the new technique. After the induction, I ask the athlete to take a deep breath before imaging performing the new technique. I suggest the athlete feel an energy filling his or her lungs and chest as the air enters. With a slow exhale, the athlete will feel the energy going to the relevant muscles while imaging the new technique. I suggest that the athlete image executing the activity several times and feeling the power that comes from that muscle or, usually, muscle group. Repeating the image several times fixes the procedure as part of the routine activity.

Shot-Putter

My work with a university shot-putter illustrates this method of mobilizing energy. Lee was interested in improving his throw. He was a football player wanting to keep in shape during the off-season. He decided on the shot put as an appropriate muscle-building activity because he had some experience with the shot put in high school, but he had not seriously worked on this event. He had enough coaching to execute the technique correctly, but he was not getting as much power from his torso and legs as he should. The coach suggested that his torso muscles were not making their contribution to his throw. While Lee was in a trance, I asked him to feel that he was absorbing energy as he took in a deep breath. As he exhaled, he would feel this energy going throughout his body—particularly to all the torso muscles he used in the throw. As he inhaled again, he would feel more energy going to those muscles, and as he exhaled the third time, he would image making the throw in slow motion. He rehearsed this image several times, each time imaging the throw a little faster and getting greater kinesthetic reactions in his torso muscles, which previously had not been fully activated in his throw.

Initially Lee was seated as we practiced inhaling and feeling the energy throughout his body. I find inducing a trance is easier when the participant is seated, so I usually begin a session that way. It was soon clear that Lee could image the throw better when standing, so he stood for the later part of this procedure. In sessions in the field where he threw the shot, standing for the hypnotic imagery was natural.

After getting more of the torso involved, we worked similarly on involving the muscles of the legs more fully in the throw. After a few images he could feel a strong input from his torso and leg muscles as well as his arms. We reinforced this in several sessions. I asked Lee to use this breathing procedure when he actually threw the shot.

Immediately after each session, he followed this new procedure in his practice throws. He commented immediately that he felt the throw coming from deep in his body, and even from down in his calf muscles. He had experienced some of this feeling before our work together, but now he felt it much more than before.

In his next meet, using this technique, he increased his distance by a little over 10 percent from his previous personal best. As he practiced this technique, his ability to inhale and feel this energy going to all the appropriate muscles improved. By being more conscious of using his whole body in the throw, he said when he actually threw he felt the throw coming from his feet right on up through his body to his fingertips. With more practice he continued to improve his distance.

Why the Technique Works

The hypnosis sessions enhance several factors at work here. Inhaling deep breaths brings more oxygen into the system and thereby more power to the muscles. Being fully aware of all the appropriate muscles increases the likelihood that they will be used. Timing a strong exertion with exhaling allows more power than an exertion with inhaling. All these contribute to increased performance.

In using this system, keep in mind the object of activating all the relevant muscles. Changes in technique are often posed as simply keeping the arm in a certain position or pointing your toes a certain way. The purpose of these changes is to get more power, but sometimes the desired effect of the change is not clear to the athlete—sometimes it is not even clear to the coach. The coach makes the recommendation because that is the way some expert does it. When the effect on the power of the exertion is explicit, the athlete is more likely to feel and produce the desired effect.

Automatic Performance

When a competent athlete performs in competition, the performance is almost automatic. When learning a technique, attention may be given to breathing, to the position of the arms, and to other details, but such thoughts do not belong in a performance. Techniques should be learned well enough that the body takes over from conscious thought. The ideal performance is so automatic that some athletes say they leave their heads behind when they compete. Techniques must be practiced enough so that they can be executed without attention. Practicing technique in a trance—either self-induced or hetero-induced—can be very effective in making that technique automatic. With the shot-putter described here, for example, I had him feel the use of all his muscles enough times in a trance that this became automatic for him.

IF YOU DON'T HAVE A DREAM, HOW YOU GONNA HAVE A
DREAM COME TRUE?
NELLIE FORBUSH'S SONG IN *SOUTH PACIFIC*

Chapter 6
Building Motivation With Goals

Setting goals and expecting their achievement—developing memories of the future—is an effective mental skill. As mentioned earlier, the unconscious and the emotional right-brain functions become more available in a trance. Thus, goals set in a trance are more useful, and the memories of achieving these goals, imprinted in a trance, can powerfully motivate an athlete. The commitment that accompanies goals and memories established in a trance can empower performance.

Importance of Goal Setting

We can compare an athlete in training to a sailboat. Although a boat or an athlete may be in good physical condition, both need a wind (motivation) to encourage movement, but the direction of the movement depends on having set the sails and the rudder (the goal) to control the direction. By controlling the sails and the rudder, a boat catches the power of the wind and uses it to go in the desired direction. Setting goals is like setting the sails and rudder. Even with great energy and enthusiasm, unless the athlete sets specific goals, that is, a direction to go, the athlete may be adrift, heading in an irrelevant direction or just flailing about.

It is clear that athletes who set specific goals improve faster than those who do not. Most coaches emphasize this aspect in training. The key is to set measurable goals that are sufficiently challenging, yet still attainable. This is easier said than done. A goal that is too easy is not motivating, and a goal that is too difficult leads to discouragement. Individual attention from the coach or psychologist can help the athlete set personally appropriate goals.

FINDING MEANING

I encountered a fine example of the value of goal setting when I met with a group of female gymnasts ages 9 to 13. As part of the getting acquainted process, I went around the circle asking each to name a specific trick she was working on. Each named one or two specific tricks, except one girl. She mumbled a bit, unable to express anything specific and finally said she really just wanted to get better. In a conversation immediately after this session, the coach said he finally realized why this girl seemed so unmotivated. Later, the coach and I helped her decide on two specific flips that she wanted to include in her floor routine. A week later the coach said he was astounded at the difference this made in her attitude during practice. The attitude improvement was noticeable not only in working on those two tricks she set as her goals but also in other parts of the training sessions. Simply setting specific, attainable targets seemed to change her whole attitude toward the practice sessions.

What Goals Accomplish

Cox (1994) lists four basic ways in which goal setting helps improve performance.

1. It focuses attention on a task. With a goal in mind, the athlete looks more closely at performance and ways to improve.
2. It mobilizes the efforts of the athlete. The athlete with a purpose devotes more effort to achieving that purpose.
3. It increases the directed persistence of the athlete. The focus and concentration make practice more interesting, and thus distractions are less compelling.
4. It promotes examining current strategies and developing new ones. An athlete with a goal in mind looks for effective ways to get to that target.

In addition to these four, achieving a specific goal, or even sensing progress toward a goal, provides effective reinforcement for the athlete. Practice sessions can be dull and repetitive. When the athlete sets and achieves interim goals, the practice sessions become more rewarding. Setting short-term goals that can be achieved rapidly is important—particularly for young athletes starting in a sport.

Keys to Goal Setting

Individuals may set outcome and performance goals and should use both short-term and long-term goals. Goals should be specific and measurable. Aiming to be a better gymnast or to run faster is too general to be effective. The goals should not only define a specific behavior or skill but also set a time by when you will achieve them. Furthermore, over time you need to regularly revise the goals and establish more challenging goals as you achieve them or modify them if you do not achieve them.

Outcome and Performance Goals

The goals might be performance goals or outcome goals. A performance goal would be a goal such as knocking 10 percent off my running time. A specific time schedule might be within two weeks. To meet the qualifying time for a league or national meet at the next competition would also be a performance goal.

An outcome goal would relate to a competition—to win the 400-meter race at next Saturday's meet. Useful outcome goals can be narrower than winning the event. Goals such as achieving five steals per game in basketball or getting five good shots on goal in soccer are examples of narrow outcome goals. As with the performance goals, outcome goals should also have a time frame. The goal should specify the meet or match at which you will realize the goal.

Performance goals are usually more effective than outcome goals, because achieving a performance is in the control of the athlete, but achieving the outcome goal depends on other competitors in the meet as well as the athlete. Performance goals in some areas are difficult to devise. Boxers, for example, have more difficulty devising performance goals than do gymnasts, but even with boxers, they should set meaningful performance goals.

WINNING, EVEN WHEN YOU LOSE

For example, a boxer may have a performance goal to land 75 percent of his punches or to use his left arm 10 percent of the time. These goals can be measured and evaluated. Thus, when boxers set performance goals, they can still achieve their goals, even when they lose their matches.

Short-Term and Long-Term Goals

Goals should include those you will accomplish in the short run as well as in the long run. Many performers specify small increments with short time frames.

INCHING TOWARD SUCCESS

A javelin thrower decided what distance he would have to get to win the district meet. The gain seemed impossible. He then calculated the weeks before the meet and determined that he would have to gain only six inches per week, which, broken down further, was only one inch per day. This one inch per day seemed achievable, but over time would achieve the goal of winning the district meet—a long-term outcome goal.

Tracking Goal Achievement

After goal setting, the athlete should keep track of progress toward the goal. Setting a specific behavior and a time schedule allows for this clear measurement of accomplishment. A goal such as that of the gymnast—to get better, with neither a measurable behavior nor a time frame—is much less effective than a strong statement of a specific behavior for her to achieve by a certain date. The javelin thrower, for example, could keep track of his progress day by day.

Revising Goals

You need to revise goals as you achieve or miss them, particularly the short-term performance goals. The javelin thrower did not need to revise his goal of one inch a day as long as he was meeting this schedule, but many short-term goals are for a specific performance rather than increments. When the time set for the goal achievement is up, you need to review the goals.

Sharing Goals

Athletes need to consider the extent to which they should share goals with other people. Generally, sharing the target with some others is beneficial. Understandably, athletes may not wish to share their goals with the teammates they intend to beat, but they might want to share them with parents and a few friends. Those with whom they share the goals can help the athletes keep the goals in mind and reinforce their achievement. To keep the goals in mind, athletes might print their goals in large type and post them inside a locker door or on a mirror at home. Being reminded of the goal frequently is useful for motivation.

I will add that because it is useful for an athlete to share goals with others, the athlete can also help other athletes by commending them as they reach their goals.

Setting Goals in a Trance

As with other training techniques, goal setting does not require hypnosis, but a trance facilitates coming up with challenging and appropriate goals. Perhaps the right brain and the unconscious have a clearer idea of capabilities than the conscious left brain. At any rate, the goals that come forth in a trance seem to be appropriately challenging and well accepted later by the conscious mind.

A trance not only facilitates better goals but also elicits more creative ways of achieving those goals. When an athlete sets difficult goals, I have found it useful to ask him or her in a trance what changes to make to achieve the goal. Often the athlete mentions changes that were not clear outside of a trance.

CROSS COUNTRY RUNNER

My work with Amy, a high school cross country runner, illustrates the value of goal setting. Amy was disappointed in her improvement rate despite a lot of hard work. The 50 members of the team raced every Wednesday and Saturday, and in each race she consistently placed 25th, plus or minus a place or two. The lack of improvement was affecting her interest in cross country running, and she was seriously thinking of quitting the team. The coach tried to be reassuring, reminding her that she was doing well as a sophomore running against juniors and seniors, that the times for all the runners were improving slightly each week, and her time was improving along with the rest. This was not enough for her. She said she was trying as hard as she could, but that her effort was not paying off. She didn't know what she could do to improve, and that discouraged her.

While in a trance, she set a goal of advancing about five places for the meet a week later. Although setting an expected place in a meet is, strictly speaking, an outcome goal, because she was competing with the same runners each week it was almost like a performance goal. Still in the trance, I asked what she would have to do to achieve this advance. I emphasized that she should think about running smart more than running hard, which had been her emphasis. She came up with several changes she could make in her running strategy. She had not thought of these changes before. I suspect that some changes she came up with had been suggested by the coach or her teammates, and although she had not acted on them, they had registered somewhere. Others, I believe, came from an unconscious or right-brained analysis of her running. It is worth emphasizing that different, and undoubtedly more, functions of the brain are available in a trance than when out of a trance. We rehearsed, that is, imaged, these changes while she was still in the trance, and in the next races she incorporated these changes in her run. She achieved the goal she had set—coming in 19th in the next week's team race.

After achieving this goal, we had another hypnosis session. In it she set a new goal for the next week—to come in at least 15th. She again thought of and rehearsed changes in her running style and effort she thought would help her achieve this goal. Although she was not able to advance as far as her goal that week, she did come in 17th, ahead of a couple more runners than the week before. I wondered whether she would be discouraged at not achieving 15th place, but she considered coming in two places better a rewarding achievement. In the next goal-setting session, she decided to get to 10th in the next two weeks. She made some further adjustments in her running style and strategy, and she was able to achieve this by her target date. I do not know where the suggestions for improvement came from, but they became available to her only during our trance sessions.

The result of the goal-setting sessions, all of which involved trances, was not only increased performance but also a runner who enjoyed her running much more. The feeling of satisfaction she received from achieving her goals was a tremendous boost to her enthusiasm for cross country running. After she achieved the first goal, there were no more thoughts of dropping off the team.

Memories of the Future

To gain the maximum effect from goal setting, athletes should be made aware of the good feelings they will realize when they achieve the goal. These good feelings can generate passion for the goal. Thus, an effective part of goal setting is having the athlete in a trance imagine having achieved the goal at some specific time in the future—to image the satisfaction of success, the glow of accomplishment. This satisfaction serves as a real motivation, a passion for achievement that will last through practices.

The phrase "memories of the future" represents this concept. If athletes establish challenging goals, then image the strong, positive feelings that will come when they achieve these goals, the goals become more empowering. Imaging the goal achievement and the feeling of pride, approval, and satisfaction on meeting the goal—developing memories of the future success—are a vital part of my goal setting with athletes. Because images are so much more vivid in hypnosis, using a trance to create images is a powerful way to develop these memories and some passion for the goal.

Effect on Motivation

Understanding the motivating power that comes from feeling successes was part of the work of McClelland (1955) in his Need for Achievement (N-Ach) studies. McClelland found that high N-Ach is characteristic of successful people. He also found that people with high N-Ach tend to not only set goals but also imagine achieving those goals and the good feelings associated with that final achievement. When a person holds these vivid images of success, the goal seems more achievable and worth the effort. Sensing the satisfactions of achieving a goal provides important motivation for an athlete.

Whenever an athlete sets goals, I follow this by guiding the athlete in a trance to image the variety of personal good feelings—all the positive internal emotions—that will accompany attaining that goal. Going beyond the personal feelings of pride and accomplishment, I encourage the athlete to sense the approval of others. If the athlete indicated an interest in the approval of the coach, parents, friends, or another person, it is effective to suggest imaging these approvals too. Include in the imagery any aspects of success that the athlete has indicated are important. The more aspects of success you can include, the more effective the image of the future. The most important feature, of course, remains the athlete's feelings of pride and accomplishment.

This imaging can help achieve both short-term and long-term goals. Reinforcement plays a big part in the motivation of any athlete. Anticipating the reinforcement from achieving the preset goals strongly supports an athlete's motivation.

Joe Montana (Montana & Weiner, 1997) encourages storing future memories in this way.

> If you are in a slump, focus on your mental approach before you mess around with what you are doing physically. Visualizing specifically and realistically what you will be doing will help you move from stressed-out to confident and relaxed. . . . This isn't fantasizing, it's rehearsal.

Effect on Confidence

Imaging success helps an athlete see achieving a difficult goal as a real possibility. This confidence motivates the athlete to expend the energy necessary to achieve the goal. After imaging success, one athlete said she knew she could make this imaged goal in the meet because she felt she had already done it.

THE 500-YARD FREESTYLER

A high school swimmer provides another example of the power of imaging the achievement of challenging goals. He competed in the 500-yard freestyle. His personal best time was 6:17, and his other recent times were from 6:17 up to 6:25. Quite consistent. His 6:17 qualified him for the district meet, which was to take place about a week after I worked with him. In a trance I asked him, "How well are you going to do in the district meet?"

"I will do it in 6. . . ," but then there was a long pause. He was obviously thinking of how many seconds to add.

I asked him again, "What will be your time in the district meet?"

Again he said "6. . .," and again a pause.

During this longer pause I said confidently, "You mean you will do it in 6 flat."

He objected to this, but I suggested that something in him was reluctant to add any seconds to the 6 flat.

He pondered this a bit. Before he had time to come up with a longer time, I continued, "Maybe there is something inside you that says you can do it in 6 flat." He pondered some more but didn't say anything. Then I asked, "What would you have to do differently to do it in 6 flat?"

"I would have to cut a second off each length." (To save the readers' calculations, the 500 is 20 lengths of a 25-yard pool.)

"How would you do that?"

"My turns would have to be faster."

"Can you do your turns a bit faster? Do you know how and will you be able to do a turn faster?"

"Yes, I know how, and I can do it."

"Would that cut a second off each length?"

"No, I don't think so."

"What else could you do to cut off that second?"

"I know I always have energy left when I finish the race, so I could put a little more power in each stroke, and I could be more streamlined when I swim."

"Would those two changes cut the second off each lap?"

With almost astonishment and real glee, "Yes, it would!"

"You will do it in 6 flat?"

"I can. . . . I will!"

I had him image doing several laps with a faster turn, being more streamlined, and putting a bit more energy into each stroke. The confidence began to come when he imaged doing these laps one second faster. I actually timed him in his imaging, and he did image each lap one second faster.

His confidence came most fully when he realized how great he would feel when (I kept insisting *when*, not if) he accomplished a 6-minute 500. He also imaged the coach's congratulations and his teammates' approval. Best of all, he knew his parents would be at the meet, and he imaged how proud and excited they would be. We spent time enjoying these memories of the future, visiting each several times. He had no trouble staying with the images of these good feelings he would have at the end of the race because these thoughts were so pleasantly exciting. The motivation engendered by these feelings was visibly intense and exciting to him. He was committed.

In the district meet he swam the 500 yards in 5:58—cutting almost exactly one second per lap off his personal best! I was happy to see that he realized all his images of approval—his future memories. I happened to be sitting near his parents at the meet. They were astounded and thrilled at his success. He had told them he would swim the 500 in 6 flat. They were surprised at his confidence but had humored him, not able to imagine that he could or would do it. I think that the images, the memories of the future success, were the potent force in driving him to a new personal best.

Uneståhl (1986a, p. 291) quotes Olympic swimmer Pär Arvidsson:

"If you have been swimming a perfect race in your inner mental room for more than a half a year then you can trust your body to do the real race in exactly the same way." Good athletes have learned to control their destiny by clear, concrete, specific, and brave multisensory images of the future.

This memories-of-the-future technique is useful for short-term goals as well as for long-term ones. The athlete must feel the satisfaction that will come from small improvements in the practice sessions—in the times for running a 400 or from small increases in the distance of a shot put or javelin throw. Having the athlete anticipate the feelings that will come when achieving the goals is an important addition to goal setting. These memories of the future can be a strong motivation for practices and competitions.

Hypnosis' Contribution to Goals and Future Memories

I conducted all the conversations in the example just cited when the swimmer was in a trance. The trance kept his focus on the meet and thus allowed me to make some suggestions, but the swimmer came up with the techniques and accepted the decisions. Imaging the effects of the success, the memories of the future, was clear and powerful for him, much more powerful than they would have been if he had not been in a trance. Hypnosis will significantly increase the vividness and effectiveness of this use of imagery.

Emphasizing the use of future memories goes against the belief that the past determines the future. Rather, our vision of the future can be a much more powerful force in determining the future than we usually give it credit for. Thus, memories of the future can be a greater influence on present behavior than memories of any past experiences.

Most coaches and athletes do not need to be reminded to set goals. However, it is not common to use the full power of the mind—left brain and right brain—by setting the goals and by pursuing ways to achieve them in a trance. Coaches who use relaxation exercises such as Suinn's VMBR might effectively set goals, work on methods of improvement, and establish appropriate memories of the future after they get their athletes relaxed.

WHEN SHE WAS GOOD, SHE WAS VERY, VERY GOOD,
BUT WHEN SHE WAS BAD SHE WAS HORRID.
FROM THE GIRL WITH THE CURL, A MOTHER GOOSE RHYME

Chapter 7
Optimizing Arousal Levels

Athletes treasure the experience of performing in the zone and they remember experiencing diminished performances when they were out of the zone. Although we may not experience the extremes of the "girl with the curl," the term horrid can apply to our feeling when we fall short of the "very, very good" performance we know we are capable of. Being in the zone is related to the level of arousal—the energy or tension the athlete feels. When this arousal is too high, the athlete makes mistakes and performance deteriorates. When arousal is too low, things don't come together and performance falters.

Arousal or Anxiety

Some sport psychologists use the term arousal and some use anxiety. Although the two terms are sometimes used interchangeably, they are not the same. Anxiety has some negative connotations that arousal does not have. Anxiety emphasizes the mental aspects of the phenomenon of concern here, and arousal emphasizes its physiological aspects. Although it is easy to associate anxiety with high arousal, it is difficult to think of anxiety associated with low levels of arousal.

Although a psychologist may use one word or the other, most theories address both the cognitive and physiological aspects of this phenomenon. Some psychologists avoid the use of arousal because of its sexual connotations, but arousal seems to me to be the most appropriate word. Anxiety is probably the more commonly used term, perhaps because there are more validated tests for anxiety than there are for arousal. In the discussion that follows, however, I will use the term of the researcher whose work I am discussing. When working with athletes, I use the term arousal. I find that the connotations of arousal, even with (or maybe because of) its sexual connotations, are more positive than those of anxiety.

To illustrate the problem that athletes may have with arousal, Weinberg and Gould (1999) describe a study in which a coach asked his 400-meter runners to run all out—to give 110 percent. A few days later he asked them to run the same distance at 95 percent. The times for the 95 percent run were better than those for 110 percent. These researchers suggest that trying for a 110 percent effort, an excess level of arousal, made the athletes tighten up too many muscles, not only the agonist muscles that help the runner but also the antagonist muscles, those opposing the agonist muscles. At 95 percent, the antagonist muscles were relaxed, which allowed the agonist muscles to operate without this resistance. Thus the effort became more efficient and they ran faster.

Yerkes and Dodson's Inverted-U

The earliest exploration of the effect of arousal was done by Yerkes and Dodson (1908). Their experiment tested the learning performance of rats with low, medium, and high arousal. They found that a medium level led to more rapid learning than either high or low arousal. They also found that the optimum arousal level was different for tasks of different difficulty, and they found a sex difference in the optimum arousal level. Their work led to the idea of the inverted-U, the starting point for most of the later theories explaining this phenomenon. Although there have been several modifications and challenges to this theory, the basic idea of the inverted-U has general acceptance—that performance increases with arousal up to some level, but arousal beyond this level interferes with performance. Later research has shown that different athletes have various best arousal levels, but confirms that each athlete has a unique optimum amount or level of arousal for best performance, and performance is diminished when arousal is under or over this level. This optimum level is now viewed as a range, that is, a zone, not a specific value.

Hanin's Zone of Optimal Functioning

Yuri Hanin (1980, 1995) has termed this optimal performance state the Zone of Optimal Functioning (ZOF) and has related it to the state anxiety of the athlete. He has measured state anxiety with a Russian adaptation of Spielberger's (1983) State-Trait Anxiety Inventory (STAI). Refining the original inverted-U hypothesis, Hanin proposed that the optimum level of anxiety is a range, specifically, a range of four points on the STAI on either side of the athlete's optimum value. He termed this optimum level of anxiety, a unique value for each athlete, the Individual Zone of Optimal Functioning (IZOF). An athlete is in this IZOF when the state anxiety is within this small range. The significance of performing at this optimum level is shown in another study cited by Hanin (1995, p. 109) in which "in an extremely important competition, 75 percent of the successful athletes were within the 64 points ZOF range and 67 percent of the less successful athletes were outside of this range." He therefore suggests that we might take the 64 range with caution—for some it might be more, for others less.

Hanin (1995) cites various research studies showing that many athletes find their optimum levels with low anxiety (38 percent in one study, 48 percent in another), others find their optimum at moderate levels (37 percent in one study, 22 percent in another), and still others find a high level optimum (25 percent in one study, 30 percent in another). This has substantial implications for coaches who attempt to get the team members to the highest possible level of arousal just before a competition.

In his 1980 paper Hanin acknowledges the problem of helping athletes achieve their IZOF in competitions. He suggests several ways to optimize the precompetition state of the athlete. These include

- controlling the subjective significance of the upcoming activity,
- increasing the athlete's confidence to successfully cope with the task,
- limiting the number of people to whom the athlete is particularly oriented, and
- creating "a desirable social environment through the regulation of communication and interaction of the partners among themselves and with the coach."

His 1995 paper deals with achieving the IZOF in only two sentences in his final paragraph (p. 116). "This model enables top performers and their coaches, managers, and applied sport psychologists to visualize and discuss possible ways to enhance performance by self-monitoring one's emotions. It provides a reality-oriented theoretical framework by which an athlete's performance and emotional experiences, both positive and negative, can be better understood and controlled more effectively through changes in short- and long-term goal setting." Although his formulations have been widely read and accepted by many applied sport psychologists, he could provide more practical suggestions about or research aimed at effecting the optimal levels of anxiety in athletes.

Somatic and Cognitive Anxiety

Several more recent theories separate the effects of cognitive anxiety and physiological anxiety. Cognitive anxiety relates to fear, apprehension, and worry about performance—the potential for damage to your self-esteem or reputation. Somatic anxiety includes physiological symptoms such as sweaty palms, increased heart rate, and shortness of breath. As we would expect, cognitive and somatic anxiety are related though not identical. Krane (1993) found the correlation to be a modest 0.67. She also confirmed that performance was best when the athlete was in the individual's zone (Hanin's IZOF). For both cognitive and somatic anxiety, performance diminished significantly when the anxiety exceeded the optimum level, and performance also diminished, but somewhat less, when anxiety was below the ZOF.

Fazey and Hardy's Catastrophe Model

Another approach that separates the two types of anxiety is the catastrophe model of Fazey and Hardy (1988). When cognitive anxiety is low, the graph of physiological anxiety versus performance is the shape of the inverted-U. When cognitive anxiety is high, the graph is like a cresting wave. Performance improves as anxiety increases, up to the peak, but soon after the peak, performance drops off catastrophically. To recover the peak state, the athlete must reduce the somatic anxiety level well below that associated with the peak to regain the composure necessary to resume the high performance level (see figure 7.1).

Another group of researchers (Gould, Petlichkoff, Simons, & Vevera, 1987) relate the two types of anxiety separately to performance. They

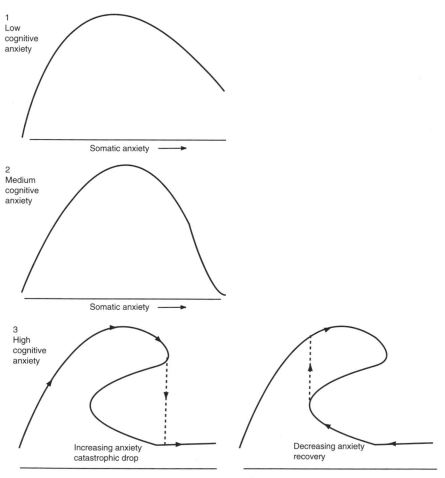

Figure 7.1 Performance versus somatic anxiety at three levels of cognitive anxiety.

have found that cognitive anxiety has a negative linear relationship to performance—as cognitive anxiety goes up, performance goes down. Only somatic anxiety has the familiar inverted-U shape.

Unestähl's Ideal Performance State

Lars-Eric Unestähl has a different approach with his Ideal Performance State (IPS). Unlike the other theories described here, he is more concerned than the others with ways to get athletes into this Ideal Performance State. He defines the IPS by listing some of its characteristics. His athletes report it is like an altered state of consciousness—almost like a hypnotic state. The athlete is intensely focused on a limited number of task-relevant stimuli and dissociated from everything except these stimuli, almost like being in a tunnel. After a good IPS performance the athlete may have little recall of the event, unlike after a mediocre performance when the athlete can remember much of the performance. Perception in the IPS changes: the action seems in slow motion, the goal post (or other target) seems larger, enjoyment is intense, pain does not exist, and the action is effortless. He quotes one athlete.

> Suddenly everything worked. I did not wonder any longer what to do or how to do it—everything was automatic. I just looked on. . . . I had no thoughts of doing it correctly, no thoughts of failure, no thoughts of fatigue. I felt an inner security and confidence that was tremendous. It was completely natural that I should succeed (Unestähl, 1986b, p. 35-36).

Unlike the researchers just mentioned, Unestähl's main concern is helping people get to their IPS. His program has been used extensively in Sweden, not only with athletes but also with school children, business executives, and others. He cites impressive results for athletes who have completed his Inner Mental Training (IMT) program. In a European championship, only one percent of the athletes had completed his IMT, yet 30 percent of the Swedish champions and 37 percent of European champions were in the IMT group. In 1980, one third of the Swedish Olympic team members had IMT training, while two thirds of the medalists had this training (Unestähl, 1986b).

Unestähl claims that the IPS can be developed and controlled most easily in an altered state. He conducts an extensive IMT program to help athletes achieve this IPS. In one of his techniques for this, the athlete enters a trance with a progressive relaxation induction. The instructions in the induction often suggest that the person go down a stairway (a deepening technique) to an "inner mental room," a comfortable place that the athlete can decorate in any personally satisfying way. Included in the room is a large screen and a blackboard on which the athlete can write. The athlete writes or describes the desired feeling for the rest of the day, for example, to be calm, relaxed, alert, or any feeling the athlete wants to achieve. Alternatively, the writing may describe some action or technique to develop or achieve. As the writing is done, an image of the athlete accomplishing this feeling or action will appear on the screen. By watching and feeling the image on the screen, the athlete will absorb the attribute or skill. One way to help athletes get to their IPS is through repeatedly rehearsing the skills and feelings involved in an IPS performance in their inner mental room.

In addition to arousal control, the IMT program emphasizes using the inner mental room to practice the skills of physical and mental relaxation, goal setting, focusing, and ego strengthening—topics covered in other chapters of this book.

Solving the Arousal Problem

I have used hypnosis in a different way to help athletes learn to control arousal and get into their zone. The method is consistent with all the preceding approaches.

Imaging a Good Performance

I ask a person in a trance to image a time when he or she performed a difficult task very well—some time when the arousal was just right, when the athlete was in the zone, or near it. When this is achieved, I ask the athlete to examine and then describe how the body feels, how the mind feels. Usually this elicits adjectives such as relaxed, strong, focused, concentrated, confident, and smooth. Encouragement to verbalize these feelings helps the athlete recognize and intensify the feelings. When the athlete has imaged and experienced the feelings at the optimum arousal, I ask him or her to see a large scale, like a giant thermometer, that reads from 0 to 200. As the athlete is at the optimum, the scale reads 100. Usually a subject has no trouble in visualizing the scale. To check on this, I often ask, "What is the color of the scale?" and, "What color are the numbers?" When the athlete gives immediate answers to these questions, I know he or she has achieved the visualizations of the scale and, more significantly, the mental state.

This is the arousal level associated with the athlete's best performance, and the one to regain when arousal differs from this level. Anchoring this feeling by grasping the person's elbow while the athlete is in a trance helps regain this feeling at later times in this procedure.

Imaging a Bad Performance

While still in a trance, I ask the athlete to image a time when arousal was too high for an effective performance—some time when excess anxiety or arousal interfered with good performance. When the athlete images that experience, I ask him or her to notice how the body and mind feel. Adjectives such as tense, worried, distracted, uncertain, and unfocused come forth. When the athlete images and describes the actual performance in that state, adjectives such as sloppy, weak, and below par come out. I ask the athlete to notice that the scale now reads 130 or 140.

Controlling High Arousal

I tell the athlete that the scale can be brought down to 100 by gradually inhaling a big breath and saying "focus," or "concentrate," or some word the subject uses to describe the optimum state. When slowly exhaling, the person is to say "relax," and as the breath goes out, the scale will come down 15 or 20 points, about halfway back to 100. It is important to use strong words such as "strength" or "focus" on the inhale and softer words such as "relax," "smooth," or "fluid" on the exhale. This is because the natural feeling when inhaling seems to be one of gaining strength, and when exhaling, of relaxation. (This seems to go against the statement made earlier that the maximum energy is available when you are exhaling. When exhaling slowly, as is appropriate here, you experience a feeling of relaxation. When you want a large burst of energy, rapidly exhaling enhances the strength of the burst.)

I often find it helpful to use physical stimuli to strengthen oral hypnotic suggestions. Here, I teach the athlete to use a few deep abdominal breaths to achieve the optimum arousal, because inhaling deeply tends naturally to make an athlete feel strong and confident, while exhaling slowly tends to reduce tension. The hypnotic suggestion helps the athlete intensify the natural feelings associated with deep breathing. As I am teaching this association, grasping the elbow is a supplemental signal to produce this desired arousal. I first grasp the elbow when the athlete has imaged being at the appropriate arousal level. Later, grasping the elbow serves as a physical signal associated with that level. Grasping the elbow is used only when I am teaching that a few deep breaths will enable the athlete to effect the appropriate arousal or to feel strength for a performance. Here, both grasping the elbow and taking a deep breath are physical stimuli which help empower a suggestion. Such physical sensations are particularly useful when an athlete can produce the physical sensation and when the physical sensation has a natural tendency to produce the desired effect.

I ask the athlete to continue the image of the event when arousal was too high while gradually bringing the scale down to the optimum level of arousal. With another deep breath or two, the scale will get to 100, and the athlete will achieve a more ideal state of mind and body. If the anchor of grasping the subject's elbow was established earlier, using this anchor as the scale gets to 100 will help reestablish the optimum feelings. I then ask the athlete to image performing again in the situation where there was trouble earlier. When the scale reads 100, that is, when the arousal is optimum, the athlete will image a performance much more satisfactory than with the arousal at 130.

It is useful for the athlete to image several instances of reducing an excessively high arousal using the deep breathing in a trance. These should include not only reducing arousal before an event but also reducing arousal during the excitement of an event—in the midst of a soccer match for example.

Increasing Arousal

In my experience, most athletes suffer from excess arousal much more frequently than from underarousal. Underarousal is rarely a problem in competition, but it is a problem for some athletes in practice sessions. When an athlete describes, or admits, trouble in getting up for some practice sessions, I reinduce a trance and ask the athlete to image such a situation. When imaging such low arousal, I suggest that the scale will read 70 or 80. I ask the athlete to inhale deeply, to say "focus" or "concentrate," and to feel energy coming in. As the athlete does this, I say that the scale will come up toward or to 100. When the athlete exhales, I suggest that this energy will spread through the body. After one or two breaths, the scale will rise to 100, and the arousal and the energy will be up to the desired level. Again grasping the elbow of the athlete will help to reinstate the optimum level.

The word "relaxed" must be handled carefully; the athlete is not to feel weak and flaccid but to feel a fluid and powerful ease or flow. I generally do not use the word relax unless I am sure that the connotation is fluidity and not weakness.

It is helpful for the subject in a trance to visualize several times when the arousal is too high and several times when the arousal is too low. The athlete should rehearse the deep breaths and the words that bring the reading to 100 enough so they are almost automatic. It is also valuable to have the athlete experience how much better the performance is when the scale is at 100, rather than at 70 or 130.

Introducing Diaphragm Breathing

Many athletes will expand their chests and suck in their abdomens when asked to take a deep breath. This is a sign for me to teach the person how to use the diaphragm in breathing. A quick physiology lesson in breathing—the role of both the rib cage and the diaphragm—helps the athlete understand that expanding the lower torso at the same time as the chest brings in considerably more air.

TEACHING DIAPHRAGM BREATHING

I suggest that this revised deep breathing will always move the body toward the 100 level of arousal and that this type of breathing will trigger the body to move the level of arousal to the optimum level. In both lowering the arousal to 100 and bringing it up to 100, I suggest that two deep breaths will bring the arousal to 100 from either direction.

Although most singers and wind instrument players learn how to use the diaphragm in breathing, athletes are seldom exposed to this idea. It is a lesson that could help many athletes. Deep breathing not only brings in more oxygen but also can be a signal that relieves excess arousal. When I started to work with one gymnast, I noted that he was taking short breaths before each event. After teaching him diaphragm breathing, I suggested that he take two or three such deep breaths before each event. He found that it calmed his nervousness and provided him with a surprising feeling of strength as he started each routine.

Theoretical Justification

Having an athlete in a trance image her own top performance to recapture that feeling of being in the zone is consistent with the inverted-U,

IZOF, and IPS theories. In each system the athlete determines her optimum level by recalling and imaging an optimum performance. Hanin determines an athlete's IZOF (Individual ZOF) by having him recall his state anxiety when functioning optimally. When he recalls this state the athlete completes the STAI. His IZOF is that score ± 4 units on the STAI scale. Hanin's research (1980) shows that an athlete's later recollection of state anxiety correlates highly (0.6 to 0.8) with the actual state anxiety at the event. Unfortunately, knowing your STAI score does not automatically allow you to recapture the appropriate state. In contrast to Hanin's procedure, Uneståhl has the athlete recall an ideal state in a trance.

Achieving Optimum Arousal

I have the athlete set the ideal state at 100 (an arbitrary figure), with the goal of reestablishing that level. There is no concern whether this 100 is a low, medium, or high value relative to other athletes. It is a value uniquely appropriate to the athlete I am working with. Asking an athlete to image the arousal level for an optimum performance and labeling that level 100 allows individual differences in arousal level. I don't try to determine whether this is low or high with reference to other athletes.

Several authors have challenged Yerkes and Dodson's inverted-U concept. The challenges generally concerned wrong assumptions that the original inverted-U theory suggested a moderate anxiety level is the single best level for all athletes, or that an optimum level for each sport exists. Yerkes and Dodson actually found different levels were appropriate for different tasks and that there were sex differences in optimum levels. Several studies, Raglin and Turner (1993) for example, refute their version of the inverted-U hypothesis by showing that not all athletes perform best at a moderate level of arousal. As Hanin has shown, the optimum level is unique to each athlete. Although it might seem that the best level for a golfer would be lower than that for a boxer, the variation between individuals is more important than any differences in the sport. All athletes, however, seem to be able to visualize a time when optimally aroused, as well as when overaroused or underaroused. I can give them posthypnotic suggestions that will usually enable them to achieve their best level.

Cox (1994) cites several theorists who have hypothesized that somatic anxiety diminishes rapidly once performance is underway but that cognitive anxiety can remain high, fluctuate, and influence the athlete throughout a performance. Therefore, the athlete must be aware that controlling the arousal level at various times during a performance is important and to get help in learning to correct the level whenever it could interfere with top performance.

Practicing controlling the arousal level at different times in a performance is an important part of the trance work. This enables an athlete to control the arousal level to achieve a consistently optimum performance.

Nonhypnotic Techniques

Athletes can modify the procedure outlined here and use it working alone without hypnosis—at least to a limited extent. They should first achieve a relaxed state, using either Benson's or Suinn's relaxation technique. In this relaxed state, they are usually able to imagine their feelings when in the zone and when overaroused. Athletes can practice reducing excess arousal by slow, deep breaths. Although suggestions made to an athlete in a trance are more powerful, an individual athlete working alone can practice the feeling of reducing the arousal and thus develop an individual method of anxiety reduction.

OVERCOMING A TENNIS SLUMP

Tennis was an important part of Jan's life. She was a lead player on her university's team. Now married and out of school about five years, she had been playing on a team sponsored by her health club. She had done well in both singles and doubles and was one of the mainstays of the team until she went through a rough time emotionally with family illness and marital difficulties. These had cut into her practice time, and her playing had been adversely affected. Although these were no longer problems, she had not been able to regain her spark and enthusiasm, and her game was not up to par.

Encouraged by another member of the team whose daughter I had helped, Jan called me. In describing her problem, Jan said she couldn't get much enthusiasm or energy in practice, so she wasn't doing well in the practice sessions. This carried over into competitive matches, where she couldn't play well because of being nervous. Her playing was obviously down from what it had been; she was losing to players she had easily beaten before her current slump.

It seemed a clear example of a lack of skill in controlling arousal. Her arousal was too low in practice sessions and too high in her matches. She still enjoyed the game and felt it kept her in good physical condition, which was obviously important to her. She believed that some work with hypnosis would help her out of her slump.

I first worked with establishing a pattern of diaphragm breathing, which she learned rapidly. She laughed at how she preferred to keep her abdomen flat, but she was willing to let it expand from time to time if it would help expand her lung capacity.

Once Jan learned to breathe correctly, she proved susceptible to hypnosis, entering a trance rapidly. In the trance she could readily image herself playing well. She felt right on, strong, smooth, and similar adjectives. She saw the scale at 100, described the color, and otherwise showed that the image was vivid for her. I anchored the image by grasping her elbow.

Then, in a trance, we went back to some recent competitions in which she had not performed as well as she knew she could. She reported feeling nervous, anxious, not ready, and uncomfortable. I suggested that the scale read about 125 or 130, and she looked at it and confirmed that it did. I asked her to tell me how she was playing, and she said "sluggish," "weak," and "ragged." I suggested that if she took a deep breath as she said "focus" she would see the scale come down halfway to 100 and would feel the competent feelings she wanted to experience. If she would take a second breath, she would see the scale come down the rest of the way to 100, and she would feel ready to play. I watched her take those two deep breaths, and, as she did, I noted a definite change in her facial expression. Before it had been flaccid, but it clearly livened up as she brought the scale down to 100. I grasped her elbow to reinforce the feeling. I asked her to continue the match to see if her game was changed, and she found it right on, accurate, and strong.

We repeated this procedure for several other less-than-satisfactory matches, and she found that she could bring herself out of these slumps with a couple deep breaths.

In our second session, I reinforced what we had done in the first session by having her again image some bad matches, then we began to work on getting up an appropriate energy for her practice sessions. She told me she noticed that she felt a lot more enthusiasm in practice after our first session. Nonetheless, she still said she could improve her practices.

We went back to image some practices that had been, as she said, "flat." I suggested that the scale probably read only about 75 or 80, and she noted that it did. I asked her how she felt in the practice session and she said "tired," and "uninterested." I suggested that if she inhaled slowly as she said "strong," she would notice her energy coming in and the scale going up. As she exhaled, she would feel relaxation and fluidity as the strength spread throughout her body. She took the breath slowly and experienced the appropriate feeling. With another breath she was back up to 100. I anchored this feeling again by grasping her elbow. She quickly felt the fatigue dissipate and her energy return. We repeated this several times until she felt that she could get herself up to an appropriate energy level when needed.

I talked to her about a week later and she said her practices had become strong. In a competition with another team she won one match and lost a close match against one of the top players in the league. Though she had lost, she felt she had played well against tough opponents.

When I checked with her again after a few weeks, she felt her old energy was back both in practices and in matches. When I asked her if she thought it would be useful for us to meet again to reinforce things, she said she felt that would not be necessary. After only two sessions she was surprised to be back where she wanted to be.

Integrating Arousal Skill Training

To many athletes, the first aspect of mental training they think of is the skill of arousal control. Most athletes are aware of times when they performed at less than their potential because they were too excited. They want to achieve the control that would allow them to perform more frequently in their zone. Thus, developing this skill is almost always a part of any extended work I do with an athlete. I include it in the case studies in part III, particularly in chapter 12, "David, the Quarterback," and chapter 15, "Jim, the Pole-Vaulter."

$P = C - D$

PERFORMANCE EQUALS CAPABILITY MINUS
DISTRACTIONS

DON LIGGETT

CHAPTER 8
ELIMINATING DISTRACTIONS

The ability to eliminate distractions, to concentrate on the relevant aspects of a situation, and to block out the irrelevant is a critical skill for an athlete. You can view the excess arousal discussed in the previous chapter as one of several focus aspects that can make an athlete's performance less than his or her capability. Hypnosis can aid an athlete in developing the several aspects of an appropriate focus during practices and matches.

Breadth of Focus

The appropriate breadth of focus is not the same in every sport and is not even the same at all times within a sport. Good basketball players, when in regular play, seem to have a broad focus—they know where all their teammates and opponents are. In contrast, when shooting a free throw, the good players block out other players and narrow their focus to the basket. Attending to other players can only be a distraction.

Similarly, a football quarterback must be able to shift his focus. The attention must first be wide enough to include several possible receivers and the defensive opponents. Using this information, his focus will narrow to the best receiver. Experienced athletes know where to direct their attention and what to ignore but sometimes have difficulty doing this.

Nideffer (1992) suggests that an appropriate focus has an internal-external dimension as well as a broad-narrow dimension. With a broad, external focus the athlete scans the environment for cues. A broad, internal dimension involves the athlete's thinking and action. A quarterback scanning possible receivers represents the broad, external focus, and his analysis of the effect of choosing various receivers is the broad, internal focus. As he makes the choice, the external focus narrows to the selected receiver and the internal focus narrows to how to throw the ball to reach the selected receiver. Nideffer says that good athletes learn to shift rapidly from internal to external and from broad to narrow.

Another important type of focus relates to keeping in mind your goal during practices and games. How an athlete focuses on and thinks of specific goals effects the strength and competence used to achieve them. Effectively dealing with all aspects of focus is important in enhancing performance.

Relation of Focus to Arousal

Weinberg and Gould (1999) and Landers (1980) propose there is a direct relationship between the breadth of focus and the level of arousal. The optimal focus comes from a medium tension. When tension is too low, the focus is too broad. Focus narrows as tension increases until high tension results in too narrow a focus. Weinberg and Gould apply this to a hockey player. When arousal is low, the player attends not only to the other players on the ice but also to the crowd and other irrelevant stimuli. With appropriate arousal, the player focuses on all the relevant players and ignores the spectators and other irrelevancies. If arousal gets too high, attention is narrowed to only a few players, and the athlete may neglect the moves of other significant players.

The theory makes sense in the hockey example but does not explain why a high level of tension destroys a free throw shooter, a bowler, or a golfer, each of whom would seem to require a narrow focus. Probably the most effective focus varies from player to player as much as does the proper level of arousal.

Foci During Performance

Gallwey (1998) suggests that whenever an athlete performs, whether in practice or in competition, there should be three foci.

1. Give your best every time.
2. Analyze each performance.
3. Have fun!

The first focus should be on executing an excellent performance, the best the athlete is capable of, each time in practice or in a competition. Players waste much practice time when they nonchalantly go through their routines. The second focus should be examining each performance to determine what you can learn from it. When the player achieves an excellent performance, the execution can be examined to determine what elements produced the excellence. If the performance was poor, what went wrong? How can the athlete eliminate or reduce the problem? The third focus is to have fun in the activity. Although not all aspects of practice are a great joy, the dominant feeling when practicing or performing should be fun. If the athlete does not enjoy the sport, the performance will not improve. The axiom of the bodybuilder, "No pain, no gain," probably does not have a universal validity.

It is obviously not necessary for an athlete to be in a trance to learn to focus, but practicing it in a trance is often helpful, especially with the analysis of the performances.

SOCCER APPLICATION

Greg, a professional soccer player, had been in a slump for the first part of his season. He had been one of the top players on the team for several years, but this season he found his play much below an acceptable standard. The coach was concerned and drastically reduced his playing time. Greg was referred to me by the training staff about a third of the way through the season. In my talk with him, Greg clearly recognized that his play was not as good as in previous years, but he could not identify any cause for the problem. He felt he was trying as hard as he ever had, but things were just not clicking for him.

Greg was active most of the year in operating a sport-related business, but had enjoyed the professional competition during the soccer season. His business was across the country from his soccer team. He was comfortable in leaving his business in the capable hands of a partner during the soccer season. Initially, soccer was a major source of his income, but as his sport business grew, the soccer pay, though increasing, became a smaller part of his income. He had been successful in combining his business and the soccer for several years, but the sport business was expanding and he missed being part of it when active with the soccer team.

My discussions with Greg indicated he felt a lack of motivation and enjoyment in his soccer performance. He seemed unable to get as fired up for games and recognized he was unlikely to be asked to return to the team next year if his play did not improve significantly. He knew he was not enjoying playing as much as he had when he was in college and in his early years as a professional, but he saw this as a result rather than a cause of his poor play.

My trance work with him was designed to change his focus. He was to lose his concern for the possibility of being fired to eliminate that distraction. He was to attend to the three foci recommended by Gallwey—to give the best performance of which he was capable; to learn something each time he played by analyzing his successes and errors; and particularly to enjoy the game, to regain the joyful attitude toward soccer that he had as a college player. He was having no trouble with the first focus—playing well, but he could not figure out what was going wrong. By recalling through hypnotic imagery the joy when he was playing in college and the early part of his professional career, he recognized the different attitude he had. Imaging present matches as fun helped him to focus on the enjoyment he could still get from the game. He decided that unless he could enjoy the game, he did not want to be on the team the next year. By being able to relax, to get rid of the tension he was under from the coach, and to focus on the fun of playing soccer, he went into later games with a different attitude. His play did improve, the coach gave him more playing time, he started to score some goals, and he regained his starting position. However, he decided his future, his real fun, came through his business, and he did not sign a contract for the succeeding season. Not all applications of sport psychology end up with the player continuing in the sport!

I have found an internal focus on having fun is most critical for many players, particularly to players who have been in a sport for many years. Participating in a sport should not be like a job (even though it is for some). If it is not fun, performance suffers. Making an athlete aware of this often rejuvenates an outlook and thus a performance.

Contribution of Hypnosis

Thinking about and adopting these three foci can certainly be done without a trance. Gallwey does not suggest a trance. Using a trance to practice these three foci when imaging practice sessions or performances can help an athlete adopt the changed focus when performing. It is often more effective to analyze a performance in a trance than otherwise. The trance also provides an effective way to introduce and establish this new procedure.

THE GREATEST DISCOVERY OF MY GENERATION IS THAT
A HUMAN BEING CAN ALTER HIS LIFE BY ALTERING
HIS ATTITUDE.

WILLIAM JAMES, AMERICAN PHILOSOPHER AND
PSYCHOLOGIST

Chapter 9
Gaining Inner Strength

The inner strength an athlete feels—what Bandura (1986) terms self-efficacy—is an important factor in performance. The classic example of a lack of confidence was the achievement of the four-minute mile. For years this was deemed physically impossible. Then Roger Bannister ran a sub-four-minute mile. Almost more surprising than Bannister's achievement is that in the next 18 months, 45 other runners ran sub-four-minute miles. What had been deemed beyond human capability became almost commonplace when Bannister demonstrated its possibility.

Building Confidence

Using the techniques described in other chapters will strengthen the ego or self-confidence of an athlete. The process of setting goals and visualizing their achievement gives power to the inner strength of an athlete, a strength that actualizes the athlete's self-confidence. The athlete will also experience an increase in inner strength and self-confidence when achieving arousal control, focusing on relevant aspects of the situation, and eliminating distractions. The examples in a previous chapter of helping gymnasts feel safe doing tricks previously associated with injuries demonstrate ego strengthening and instilling self-confidence. In general, it is appropriate to include ideas about self-confidence when working with athletes on other problems.

Several suggestions made to athletes in a trance will enhance their self-confidence and thus their capabilities. These include suggestions that they will continue to improve their skill and that they will be more comfortable in their sport, mentally calmer, more alert and energetic, and less easily upset. Additional suggestions may be tailored to problems the athlete reveals in or out of the trance state.

Power of Self-Talk

Another aspect of focus relates to a player's self-talk. Many athletes, particularly young athletes, are not aware of how much a performance is affected by their internal dialog—the self-talk. Gallwey (1998) claims that doubt is the real enemy of a good performance.

DEMONSTRATING THE POWER OF SELF-TALK

The power of self-talk is easy to demonstrate by an exercise called muscle testing. This technique requires two persons—an athlete and a tester. The athlete decides on some target for an upcoming practice or event—a new personal best for a swimmer, a better free throw percentage for a basketball player, or a specific play for a football player.

The athlete holds his or her arm straight out and parallel to the floor, in line with the shoulders, and keeps the arm as stiff as possible. The tester stands facing the arm, one hand on the athlete's shoulder and one on the extended hand. Figure 9.1 illustrates this position. The tester makes a base measurement by seeing how much pressure is necessary to force the hand down about six inches.

In the first test, the tester asks the athlete to say and think, "I don't know whether I will be able to swim my event in x seconds (or whatever target the athlete selected earlier), but I hope I can." The tester again applies pressure on the athlete's wrist and notes how much pressure is needed to push it down the same six inches or so.

In the second test, the tester asks the athlete to say and think, "I will try to swim my event in x seconds." Again the tester pushes on the wrist to determine if more or less force is needed to push the athlete's arm down the same amount.

In the final test, the tester asks the athlete to say and believe, "I will swim my event in x seconds."

For most athletes, the progression from doubting to trying to performing will each produce a stronger arm than the

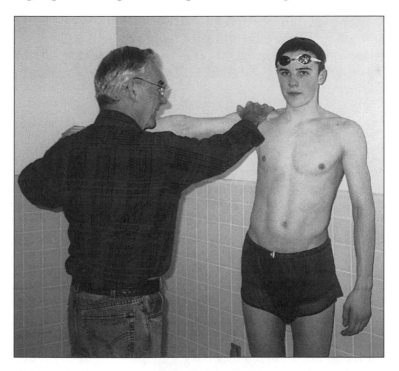

Figure 9.1 The position for muscle testing.

previous test. To further demonstrate the power of language, the tester can ask the athlete to go back to the try or doubt statements and again test the strength. The strength with these statements will be less than with the "I will" statements. In this technique, both the tester and the athlete will feel the increased strength as the statements become more positive.

Because the strength difference is so great, athletes often doubt that I am using the same pressure when they say the "try" or "will" statements. When this happens, I usually get two teammates to test each other. This also helps to convince two, rather than just one!

The effect on a person's strength from this change in the thought processes is usually a surprise, particularly to young athletes. It is difficult to overemphasize the importance of the athlete's thinking process just before an event. The athlete should make appropriate self-talk part of the routine before an event. Rehearsing this in a trance with an appropriate posthypnotic suggestion will help to establish this behavior pattern.

I follow this test by additional work to help athletes develop strong statements they can make to themselves at various times during the day, as well as just before and during performances.

Expanding Goals

Hypnosis can help convince athletes to expand their goal horizons. Visualizing previously unimagined successes can be a strong spur to achievement. Chapter 6 suggests that goals set under hypnosis are likely to be challenging and appropriate ones. Although this is generally true, athletes often need encouragement to set higher goals. Coaches are usually good judges of capability, but ultimate capability is unassessable and is probably more often underestimated than overestimated. (Parents' estimates of capabilities may be an exception to this statement!)

Dealing With Failures

Many athletes are bothered excessively by past failures. They can feel that effect both during that match and in subsequent matches. When an athlete makes a mistake during a match, the focus must be on the future and not on the mistake. My most vivid memory of a Masters professional golf tournament was seeing the man who had been 1st or 2nd all through the match take three strokes to get out of a sand trap on the 14th hole. On each of the next four holes he took one more stroke than the leader, falling from 1st place to 10th, and then off the leader board. Learning to dismiss errors and mistakes (or in this case, unfortunate failures) during a match is a skill not even senior professionals have mastered.

Sometimes losing a match can affect the outlook for future matches. Often brooding about a specific past failure or failures interferes with the athlete's confidence. The athlete can ease the pain of these failures by considering each failure as an opportunity to learn, to examine the failure as a way to improve performance and self-confidence. Gallwey (1998) recommends viewing each performance as a learning exercise. This analysis will not help a player during the match in which he or she made the error, but it will help in future matches. Though you may lose a competition, you don't have to lose learning the lesson.

An athlete whose performance in a meet was below expectations can be asked in a trance to go back in time and image the event and examine how the performance was different from times the athlete was successful. External imagery is often more useful than internal imagery, but either can be effective. Usually the recall in a trance is clearer than an individual could achieve otherwise, and this clarity will reveal problems and actions the athlete can take to perform better next time.

Too often athletes will be haunted by an error made during a match, producing a devastating effect on their performance in the rest of the match and even in future matches. Athletes should be encouraged to always look forward during their performances, rather than look back at mistakes. There is time after the match to review the failures as learning experiences.

Learned Optimism

Martin Seligman's (1990) formulation of optimism and how to increase it can be useful to athletes. He measured the optimism of individual athletes and teams and found more optimism associated with stronger performances. In his formulation, optimism is defined in terms of the attributions an individual makes to explain success and failure. Attribution theory says that humans need to explain why events happen. We do this by making attributions—finding or inventing causes for an event. The attribution is not necessarily the real reason an event occurs, but it is the way a person interprets the cause of the event. Because thought processes are important to a performance, and because they can be modified in hypnosis, Seligman's suggestions can be relevant.

He suggests that the attributions of interest are on three dimensions. The first is a permanent-temporary dimension. An example of a permanent attribution would be, "I can never do well in a competition." A temporary attribution would be, "I couldn't do well that day." The permanent attributions are seen as unchangeable, but the temporary ones may change over time.

The second dimension is a pervasive-specific dimension. A pervasive example would be, "I don't do well in any track events." A specific attribution would be, "I don't do well in short relay events." The pervasive attributions apply to all aspects of a situation, and the specific ones apply to only one or a few aspects.

The third type of attribution is a personal-external dimension. A personal attribution would be, "I wasn't feeling well that day," and an external one would be, "The competition was really tough that day."

People make attributions to explain successes as well as failures. An athlete might attribute winning a race to luck (a temporary, specific, external attribution) or to skill and training (a permanent, pervasive, personal attribution).

Optimism Versus Pessimism

Seligman says that optimists and pessimists make different attributions for their success and failure. An optimist attributes success to good factors that are permanent, pervasive, and personal. Thus an optimistic athlete expects success and is likely to attribute it to a friendly, cooperative world and to the athlete's personal efforts. "I've worked hard, and my coaches and teammates are very supportive." Success confirms the athlete's attributions about these causes and strengthens future performances. In contrast, the pessimist sees successes as caused by temporary and external factors, such as, "That was my lucky day," and to other persons, such as, "The competition was weak." The pessimist does not receive the reinforcement from success that the optimist receives.

Unlike the success attributions, an optimistic athlete would attribute a failure to a temporary or specific factor (maybe due to that day's condition of the track), or to an external factor (an equipment failure). With these attributions, the failure does not diminish the optimistic athlete's confidence for future performance.

Failures to the pessimist, on the other hand, are caused by personal, permanent, and pervasive factors, such as, "I can never do well in any track meet." Thus to an optimist a success is a self-fulfilling prophesy and to a pessimist a failure is a self-fulfilling prophesy (see table 9.1).

Seligman's (1990) book provides a test of optimism and pessimism with scores suggesting how one attributes success and failure on each of these three dimensions. It is also possible to sense the attributions that the athlete associates with success and with failure by talking to him or her about past successes and failures. If an athlete seems to score or to think in pessimistic dimensions, Seligman suggests that he or she can be helped to view successes and failures in more optimistic attributions.

The effect of these attributions on self-confidence is cumulative. All the attributions can be self-fulfilling prophesies. An athlete who succeeds and believes success is the result of personal efforts and permanent and pervasive good aspects of the environment will have these views reinforced by success. Similarly, an athlete who attributes successes to temporary and specific factors and to other people will not be as reinforced by a victory. Failure will be discouraging to a pessimistic athlete because it is attributed to some personal deficiency and to permanent and pervasive environmental factors. An optimistic athlete will not be so bothered by a failure because it can be dismissed as caused by something temporary, specific, and beyond control. Defeat will damage the outlook of a pessimistic athlete much more than that of an optimistic athlete.

Seligman does not, of course, endorse total optimism. A total optimist would have trouble seeing and correcting problems in a bad performance. As discussed earlier in this chapter, analyzing a failure for its true causes can be of great help in overcoming problems. It is important

Table 9.1   Attributions

	For success	For failure
Optimist	Permanent, pervasive, personal	Temporary, specific, external
Pessimist	Temporary, specific, external	Permanent, pervasive, personal

for self-improvement to maintain a balance between optimism and taking responsibility for your performance. Neither a totally optimistic nor a totally pessimistic attitude leads you to examine realistically your problems with any hope of improvement.

Ellis' Rational-Emotive Therapy

Some psychologists propose a theory but do not suggest how to implement the theory to help solve real problems. Seligman's views on optimism and pessimism seem to be a powerful way of viewing successful and unsuccessful athletes. Fortunately for sport psychologists who are interested in helping athletes and understanding their problems theoretically, Seligman suggests how to change these destructive pessimistic attributions by using the ideas of Albert Ellis (Ellis & Bernard, 1985). Ellis provides a way for a sport psychologist to help an athlete recognize the destructive attributions—to dispute the falsely pessimistic ones and energize more optimistic ones.

Many attributions are within the athlete's unconscious level. As discussed earlier, the unconscious motivations are much more available and docile in a trance than in the normal waking state. Hypnosis can open the way to modifying unduly pessimistic attributions. The first step is to listen to how the athlete explains—attributes a cause to—good and bad performances. Are failures caused by pervasively bad personal attributions and are the successes reinforcing to the athlete? If the athlete tends toward pessimism, which you can determine by listening to the athlete or using Seligman's Optimism/Pessimism test, then Ellis' Rational Emotive Therapy (RET) provides a path to more optimistic and successful ways of thinking.

Ellis' RET technique uses an A B C D E framework to help an athlete examine and change the attributions that would harm performance and to strengthen the attributions that enhance performance. Briefly, A is the Activation that appears to produce C, a Condition. After a defeat (A) for example, an athlete might be discouraged (C). Ellis says it is not the defeat that causes the discouragement but B, the Belief of the athlete. If this belief is a negative, permanent, pervasive, or personal attribution, the athlete can be helped to Dispute (D) the attribution and to Energize (E) a temporary, specific, external belief about the cause of the defeat. Realism should, of course, govern the attributions—the athlete should be willing to accept the real reasons for the failure. The case study of "David, the Quarterback" in chapter 12 illustrates this technique more fully.

Ego-Strengthening Scripts

Several scripts are available for ego strengthening (Hammond, 1981; Hartland, 1971; Uneståhl, 1995). In each of these the athlete images a pleasant, relaxing place. Uneståhl has the person image a room. Hammond and Hartland suggest imaging a pleasant place that could be indoors or outdoors. I suggest the athletes pick their own places, and they usually pick a pleasant place that is outdoors.

After the athlete is relaxed and enjoying this pleasant place, each author includes a variety of strengthening suggestions. Although these scripts are not specifically for athletes, you can easily adapt them to fit your needs. Uneståhl includes suggestions that you "will feel stronger in every way, both physically and mentally, more alert, more wide awake, less easily tired or bored, more deeply interested in what you are doing." Hammond has the person "allow yourself to experience good feelings of safety, happiness, competence, and calm," and later he asks the person to allow these feelings "to flow all through you, to all parts of you, allowing all of you to experience these soothing feelings." He suggests that in this pleasant place, things can come into proper perspective and the person's unconscious will know what is needed and will reveal some of it. "It may be that you hear a still voice, maybe a voice in your mind or seeming to come from deep within you, saying what you most need to hear, giving you the suggestions you most need to receive right now." He suggests that when the person comes out of the trance these feelings will remain. The athlete is encouraged to rein-force the suggestions by self-hypnosis. Hartland's script makes the same suggestions but emphasizes that the athlete will continue to improve the abilities mentioned in the trance. "Each day you will be more confi-dent in your ability to be your best self, more in control, more able to do what you really want to do. More able to hold your own."

Because inner strength is so often a problem with athletes, these ego-strengthening scripts can be effective as a complement to other tech-niques.

PREPARING FOR SCRIPT USE

The script can follow any basic induction or can follow other trance procedures. The text is only a suggestion. It should be modified to fit the therapist and the athlete.

The first step in using this script is to talk to the athlete about his or her experiences in the sport. During these conversations, the athlete will let me know where I might assist. Frequently the athlete will indicate some times or areas when he or she felt a lack of confidence or strength—some areas or times when his or her self-efficacy needed strengthening. Probing these areas may be necessary, and you can work these needs into the script at the points indicated.

This following general script can be effective when a participant is either relaxed or in a trance. The pace of the script should be slow, with plenty of pauses to allow the person to absorb and react to the suggestions. Repetition and elaboration on the ideas or statements is appropriate. It is effective to inject the participant's name often—I have suggested some of these spots by an asterisk, *.

Before using this exercise, I usually see if the person uses his or her abdomen and diaphragm in taking a deep breath. If the deep breaths involve only the upper chest, I find it useful to teach diaphragm breathing. I remind the athlete to use this deep breathing whenever I ask for a deep breath.

Insertions in italics and parentheses are to guide the therapist while reading the suggested script and are not to be read to the athlete.

Sample Script
As you find yourself relaxing, *, you are in a beautifully pleasant place. It is probably outdoors. There is some water nearby and some trees. With each breath you take, notice how your body is becoming more and more relaxed, *. Take a couple deep breaths, and as you exhale feel your whole body pleasantly relaxing. Your waist is relaxed, your legs are so relaxed they feel heavy against the chair. You look up at the sky—it is a beautiful blue with a few scattered clouds floating by. Maybe you can hear some pleasant sounds; the sounds may be from a light wind in the trees or they may be from the water. *(Leave time for the athlete to hear the sounds.)* The sun feels comfortable and warm on your face or back. *(When you ask a hypnotized person to imagine multiple sensory inputs, the imagery and the trance deepen.)* You can talk, *, without coming out of your restful relaxation. I would like you to tell me something, *, about this relaxing place. Where are you? What can you see? *(It is usually possible at this point for a person to answer questions about the pleasant place, near an ocean, a lake, or*

a stream, for example. The speech may be slow or a bit slurred, but understandable. Your further elaboration on the scene depends, of course, on the place selected. Here we will assume it is an ocean beach, which is a common choice.) Notice the sound of the breakers and how relaxing that sound is. *(Leave time.)* Perhaps you can feel the cool ocean breeze . . . , and at the same time you feel the warmth of the sun on your face or back . . . . Just inhale the smell of the fresh ocean air.

(At this point the ego-strengthening suggestions can begin.)

As you take in a deep breath, *, you feel a strength and power coming into your body. It is a strength that has always been there. Sometimes you have known it was there, but at other times you have not felt it was there for you . . . . As you take some deep breaths, you feel that strength more clearly inside you, *, small at first, but gradually expanding through your whole body and mind as you continue to breath deeply. Each time you take a deep breath you feel stronger both physically and mentally, more able to know that you have the courage and strength to do the things you want to do, more able to face the important challenges in your life, and more in control of what is surrounding you.

As this strength expands in your body and mind, you also find yourself feeling calmer, more competent, less tense or stressed, more worthy of the respect and the admiration of those you come in contact with, *. *(At this point the athlete is probably breathing normally again. If not, you can suggest that he or she just breathe normally, but that each time the athlete inhales, he or she will feel this strength.)* You find the strength and good feelings expanding to all parts of your mind and body, pervading your whole being. Just allow yourself to experience these good feelings,*. *(Pause.)* As you relax in this pleasant place, you can feel a strengthening of those areas where you want to be stronger, where you may have felt unnecessarily weak.

(Here you can insert some areas discussed with the athlete earlier.) You find that you are more able to _____. *(Fill in needs expressed earlier.)*

In the days to come, you will be able to regain this strength and these good feelings by closing your eyes and taking a couple big, deep breaths. As the air fills your chest and abdomen, you will feel this strength filling your body and mind; the calmness, the confidence, the control will be with you.

(At this point you can address more specific suggestions about areas of individual need. You may encourage the athlete to suggest some areas where a change was desired. It might be confidence at a meet, mastering some specific difficult technique, improving relationships with other players or the coach, or any other area in which a need for strength was suggested.)

Now, *, I would like you to see yourself sometime tomorrow *(or at some later date or in a situation appropriate to an earlier expressed individual need)*. You are remembering the strong feelings you have now and you wonder if you can feel them again. As you imagine yourself tomorrow, *, take a deep breath or two and feel these good feelings and strength filling your body and mind. They are available to you whenever you want them. They have always been inside you and around you, *, even though you have not always been able to feel this strength and confidence when you have wanted or needed them. Now you can; simply by taking these deep breaths you will feel the confidence that you can do the things you want to do. You say to yourself, "I can do this." *(You can fill in some action of concern to the athlete. You may have already demonstrated the value of positive affirmations described earlier in this chapter.)*

(It is often useful for the athlete to image a return to some time when confidence was lacking and to use the procedure to feel an appropriate strength.) Now I would like you to go back to _____ . *(Select an appropriate time when confidence was lacking.)* Notice how your body feels; perhaps it is somewhat tense, nervous, or uneasy. Please describe for me how your body and your mind feel. *(Pause for reaction.)* How was your performance when you felt that way? *(Pause for response.)* Now take one or two big, deep breaths and feel how this changes the way your body feels—how you regain your composure, your strength, and your ability to function up to your capacity. *(Tailor the changes you suggest to some time or event when the athlete felt a lack of appropriate composure or strength. It might be effective for the athlete with the feeling of strength to complete the event where the weakness was felt. With an appropriate suggestion, the athlete will usually image a superior performance.)* Tell

me how your body feels differently now. Say to yourself, "I can do this." See how much more effectively you can act when you have this strength. *(Pause for response.)*

In the days to come, you will be able to take these deep breaths several times each day. As you do, *, you will find yourself feeling more able, more confident, more together, more worthy of respect, more in control of yourself and what you are doing. You will find that you will enjoy drawing forth these good feelings by taking these deep breaths several times each day.

(This is the end of the script.)

Following Up
After the script you can discuss with the athlete the importance of practicing the procedure and of meeting again to reinforce the script in a later session so that the strength and good feelings will be available whenever the athlete faces an important challenge.

Hypnosis for Ego Strengthening

Often the negative beliefs that interfere with good performances are buried in the athlete's unconscious mind. Because these beliefs become more available in a trance, a skillful sport hypnotist will be able to elicit the controlling attributions more easily using a trance than in casual conversations. The trance also allows the psychologist to challenge any negative and harmful attributions and to elicit suggestions for more useful beliefs. I have found that most athletes have the key to their own better performance. As mentioned earlier, these may come from parts of the mind not accessible in ordinary conversations. The appropriate suggestions for better attributions are more likely to come from the athlete than from me and seem more likely to come out in a trance than otherwise.

Although trance work is useful here, I have found it appropriate to discuss the attributions with the athlete both before and after the trance. Often, important attributions are made at the conscious level, and you can use Ellis' methods without a trance. Ellis' methods allow the athletes to make the most effective attributions part of their self-talk.

PLEASURE IS OFT A VISITANT, BUT PAIN CLINGS
CRUELLY TO US.

JOHN KEATS, *ENDYMION*

CHAPTER 10
EASING PAIN

Most athletes are familiar with the ability of a football player to continue playing even though injured. Often the athlete does not feel the pain of an injury until after the excitement of the game. This ability of the mind to control the degree of suffering from an injury is an example of its power. What hypnosis does is to tap into this power to reduce the suffering from an injury.

Pain Control by Hypnosis

In the early 1800s several English physicians rediscovered and used the anesthetic powers of hypnosis for surgery. James Esdaile, a British surgeon, conducted several thousand surgeries in India with hypnosis as the only anesthetic. Although many other physicians were also able to use hypnotism for surgical anesthesia, the British medical establishment was reluctant to acknowledge its effectiveness. With the advent of ether and other chemical anesthetics in the mid 1800s, the use of hypnosis as an anesthetic seemed unnecessary. Chemical anesthetics have an advantage over hypnosis in that the reaction to them is more predictable than the reaction to hypnosis. Hypnosis has the advantage, however, of avoiding any side effects—no allergic reactions or other side effects of chemical anesthetics.

The ability of a person in a trance to reduce pain is familiar to people acquainted with hypnosis. I have probably been asked to use hypnosis for pain relief more often than for any other purpose. It is often the entree to using hypnosis to help athletes in their performance in other ways.

EXPERIENCING THE POWER OF HYPNOSIS

My first experience with using the power of hypnosis was with pain control. I had just returned from my first hypnosis training program—an intensive beginner and intermediate workshop sponsored by the American Society for Clinical Hypnosis (ASCH). This ASCH workshop attracted me because I had little knowledge of hypnosis, and several psychology courses I was teaching included references to the technique. Psychology students were always curious about hypnosis, and my inability to satisfy their interest made me feel guilty. I thought the workshop would allow me to become more competent in that part of my teaching. I had no idea how extensively I would become involved with hypnosis. I certainly had no plan to become a hypnotherapist.

The Monday after the ASCH course, I was visiting our athletic training room. Our college quarterback, Bart, had injured his right knee in Saturday's game and had been on crutches since. Because of the pain, Bart had not been able to put any weight on that leg or to straighten the knee. The trainer told me Bart was scheduled for a general anesthetic for the next day to examine the knee. With the general anesthetic, the physician would be able to move the leg around to test whether all the ligaments were still properly connected. When I was told that the general anesthetic was to relax and anesthetize the leg, I connected that relaxation and pain control are possible under hypnosis, and I had just learned how to do this. I immediately sensed an opportunity to find out whether the money I had spent to learn hypnosis was well spent. Could I hypnotize Bart and eliminate the pain so the trainer could move his leg around?

Bart had been in a couple of my classes and knew me well enough to feel that I was not completely off my rocker when I suggested hypnosis, so he was willing to let me try the technique. Exuding confidence, but with carefully concealed trepidation, I went ahead with an induction and relaxed and anesthetized the leg. Bart proved to be susceptible, and our head trainer was able to manipulate the relaxed and anesthetized leg enough to determine that the tendons and ligaments were all intact. The trainer's manipulation included a great deal of flexing and twisting the leg, which would have been excruciatingly painful had Bart not been in a trance. After the test I was not sure who was more astounded—Bart, the trainer, or I. None of us had ever seen hypnosis used in this way. About 10 other members of the football team witnessed the demonstration, and they began asking questions about what else could be accomplished by hypnosis. Perhaps they were intrigued by the possibility of being hypnotized, but they actively encouraged me to use hypnosis for many other sport applications. I was serendipitously started on the road to becoming a sport psychologist!

Advantages and Problems in Hypnotic Pain Control

As with many uses of hypnosis, pain relief has significant ethical and practical issues. Pain is a useful symptom, and before manipulating pain we need to recognize that it is usually the body's warning to avoid certain movements. Any time I work with an athlete on pain reduction,

I work in conjunction with the physician or athletic trainer who is treating the injury. It is important that my work complement any treatment the athlete is receiving.

Using drugs to reduce pain is an accepted part of rehabilitation, and hypnosis can usefully complement or substitute for drugs in the pain-reduction aspect of the rehabilitation. Hypnosis often reduces or eliminates the need for chemical pain relievers and thus reduces the possibility of side effects. With hypnosis, it is possible not only to reduce pain almost immediately but also to give posthypnotic suggestions that the athlete can use later, whenever the athlete would normally use a chemical pain reliever. With some athletes, it is also appropriate to teach self-hypnosis for easing later pain symptoms.

While it is frequently useful to diminish the pain level, it is clearly unethical to use hypnosis to eliminate pain so that an athlete can compete—and possibly cause irreparable further injury.

When an athletic injury requires pain relief, I do not usually give suggestions for the complete relief of the pain. Although excruciating pain is unnecessary and can be helped, some minor remnant helps keep the patient interested in continuing the appropriate treatment procedure.

My initial session with Bart was to completely anesthetize his leg so the trainer could manipulate it. In a later session I worked with Bart to help him control the pain, which was still a problem. I gave him a posthypnotic suggestion that when he felt an uncomfortable amount of pain in his knee he could close his eyes, take a deep diaphragm breath, and ease the pain. I suggested that the pain would not completely disappear, but it would get down to a much more comfortable level. While he was still in a trance, I had him image a time when he had considerable pain in his leg, then reduce this pain by taking such a breath. I repeated this several times. He later reported that this was a valuable technique. He could get an intense pain down to a tolerable level.

Although beyond the usual application in athletics, some surgeons feel that when hypnosis is substituted for chemical anesthetics in surgery or parturition, the infection rate and the recovery time are less. When the person is in a trance, suggestions can be made for a speedy recovery (see chapter 11) as well as a reduction of the pain. For a susceptible person with an appropriate therapist, hypnosis is safer than a chemical pain reliever; hypnosis has no side effects and it activates no allergies, drug reactions, or drug dependencies. However, the variation in individual susceptibility to hypnosis and the time required to teach hypnosis makes hypnosis a less preferred anesthetic procedure than the more common chemical anesthetics.

Types of Pain

Barber (1996) describes three types of pain.

1. Acute pain
2. Chronic benign pain
3. Chronic recurring pain

Acute pain is pain due to an immediate trauma—a fracture, bruise, or severe laceration. He suggests that both hypnosis and chemical agents help relieve acute pain.

The second type of pain he labels chronic benign pain. Typical examples of this would be suffering long after healing should have occurred. The sufferer has learned to maintain the pain, often because of some secondary gain. Occasionally an injured person will realize some gain from the injury or pain—sympathy, being excused from burdens, or some other advantage. This gain from the injury is called secondary gain. Simple hypnosis does not ease chronic benign pain. It requires a more complex treatment because the individual needs to understand and deal with the gain from the pain. By understanding the nature of the gain, a qualified therapist can begin an appropriate education or retraining to eliminate this secondary gain. Hypnosis' ability to work with unconscious motivations can help the therapist and the sufferer understand and deal with the psychological roots of the continuing pain. Eliminating secondary gain should be attempted only by people with solid psychological training. I describe an example of helping an athlete recover from this type of pain in the section on psychosomatic disease in chapter 11, "Unleashing Self-Healing."

The third type of pain Barber termed chronic recurring pain. This is the persistent pain typically associated with cancer or arthritis. An athlete recovering from a severe injury might suffer from pain of this type. Hypnotic treatment can be effective with chronic recurring pain.

With athletes, the first and third types of pain are the most likely. In dealing with acute pain, a therapist can induce a trance and reduce or remove the pain immediately, probably more rapidly than a chemical anesthetic would take effect.

With chronic recurring pain, through either posthypnotic suggestions or self-hypnosis, most athletes can be taught a signal to reduce intolerable or unnecessary pain. Later sessions with Bart achieved this pain reduction during the recovery from his injury. Because I generally make suggestions for healing along with suggestions for pain relief, I include more details of the techniques for suggesting pain relief in the next chapter.

Physical and Affective Aspects of Pain

Barber makes another useful distinction when he separates the physical aspects of pain from the affective aspects. The physical aspect is the intensity of the pain. The affective aspect is the felt suffering—the extent to which the pain bothers the person. This is sometimes referred to as the distinction between pain and suffering. A minor physical pain can be unpleasant for some people. On the other hand, others tolerate severe pain relatively comfortably. Before reducing any pain, it is useful for the therapist to assess not only the type of pain (acute, benign, or recurring) but also the affective response to the pain. Both affect how to deal with the pain.

Hypnosis for Pain Relief

It is sometimes helpful to provide an athlete with an example showing that the mind determines how much suffering occurs from a pain. Most will be familiar with the way football players sometimes continue to play after a serious injury—unconsciously suppressing the pain during a game, feeling the extent of the injury only after the excitement of the competition is over. The way the mind suppresses such a pain during a competition is similar to how hypnosis can help the mind suppress a pain at other times.

Using self-hypnosis for pain relief allows control of the amount of suffering. This control not only lowers the suffering directly but also gives the person a satisfying feeling of control.

PAIN AND TENSION

As described in chapter 3, pain and tension are often closely related. You can often achieve pain relief by tension relief. A teenage gymnast I will call Jennifer had a back pain that had bothered her for several weeks. It did not seriously interfere with her practice but was a lingering, annoying ache. She had been to a physician who determined that there was no physical damage but that muscle tension was the main cause of the persistent pain.

I had worked with Jennifer on other aspects of her gymnastics, so I was able to help her into a trance rapidly. We did some extra relaxation exercises to deepen her trance so she felt her body quite relaxed. Because the physician had identified the tight muscles for her, she was able to focus particularly on those muscles as I asked her to relax. They were especially tight, so at first she found it challenging to relax that area. She was soon able to visualize a relaxation in those muscles. When she felt the relaxation in those muscles, she felt the pain dissolve.

I worked with her on some self-induction procedures so she could relax those muscles during the day whenever she felt any pain or tightness in that area. I urged her to use self-hypnosis to relax that area before she went to sleep at night. (See chapter 1 for information on teaching self-hypnosis.) We talked about how important it was to keep those muscles relaxed, not only to ease pain but also to heal her body more readily.

She followed this procedure, and when I talked to her a week later, the pain was almost gone. I urged her to continue regularly relaxing that part of her back, allowing any healing that she might need, even though she felt it was not necessary for pain relief. After several weeks she was experiencing no pain in her back but enjoying self-hypnosis to get a pleasant feeling of relaxation at bedtime.

Being able to control your environment and yourself is a powerful source of comfort and satisfaction. Pain is more bearable when the victim feels some degree of control over it. Hypnosis cannot always reduce all of a recurring pain, but by giving the person some control, it can make the pain more bearable. Because pain and injury are so often associated, the next chapter will deal more with healing.

THE PHYSICIAN IS ONLY NATURE'S ASSISTANT.

GALEN, GREEK PHYSICIAN

CHAPTER 11
UNLEASHING
SELF-HEALING

The original uses of
the hypnotic trance
were for healing.
From the sleep
temples of classical
Greece, which seem
to have used a
trance for healing, to
Mesmer's work in
18th century Paris,
healing was the
overriding purpose
of the trance. Mod-
ern hypnosis contin-
ues to help individu-
als mobilize their
own healing powers.

Power of Self-Healing

Recently the power of the individual for self-healing is becoming more recognized. Herbert Benson's (1996) *Timeless Healing: The Power and Biology of Belief* is a good example of this recognition. Much of contemporary alternative medicine emphasizes the psychosomatic nature of illnesses. Enlisting the aid of the patient in bringing about healing is becoming recognized as an effective technique, and hypnosis has a long history of energizing the healing forces within an individual.

Psychosomatic Defined

The first reaction of many athletes when suggesting the use of hypnosis in healing is that their problem is strictly physical, not psychosomatic. Marlene Hunter (1987) provides a valuable explanation for those concerned with having their dis-ease called psychosomatic. Hunter says that too often when we use the term psychosomatic, the reaction is that you are saying the dis-ease is in the client's head. Hyphenating disease emphasizes that the illness is a mental discomfort.

DEFINING PSYCHOSOMATIC

Psychosomatic comes from two Greek words—*psycho* means mental or spirit, and *soma* means body. To call an ailment psychosomatic means that it has causes and effects from both mind and body. The symptoms produce dis-ease, which is a mental effect. If there were no dis-ease, you would sense no problem.

Although we generally recognize that some diseases have strong psychological elements in their origins, Hunter emphasizes that the body and the mind are in constant interaction. If a physical problem does not cause dis-ease (i.e., is not reflected in our minds), we rarely seek help for it. Thus, to Hunter, all illnesses are psychosomatic. However, she does acknowledge that a disease can exist without dis-ease. For example, women get a Pap smear to find out if they have the disease cancer before they experience any dis-ease.

Physiological and Psychological Causes

Although most athletic injuries have strictly physiological causes, some problems have psychological components. Whether psychological or physical, however, the athlete can effectively use mental powers in speeding the cure. Ievleva and Orlick (1991) found that positive self-talk, goal setting, and healing imagery enhance recovery from athletic injuries. Hypnosis is valuable in mobilizing these curing forces within the athlete and uncovering psychological elements in problems that seem strictly physical. Although there is a continuum among psychological and physiological aspects of medical problems, the following discussion will deal with ailments at both extremes and at the middle of this spectrum.

Psychological Origins

Psychotherapists have long used hypnosis in uncovering the psychological origins of physical complaints. In hypnosis, the unconscious and its hidden motivations are much more available to appropriately trained therapists, and they can tap this availability with athletes. Often there is a secondary gain that prolongs the symptom long after eliminating its cause. Barber (1996) calls this chronic benign pain (see chapter 10, "Easing Pain"). This ferreting out underlying psychological origins is a familiar tactic in psychotherapy. Using hypnosis to uncover hidden motivations in athletic disabilities is less frequent. In neither of the following cases did the coach or trainer suspect that the origins of the problems were psychological.

CASE ONE: PAINFUL CALF MUSCLES

This case is an example of using hypnosis to uncover a psychological source of a problem. John, a college football player, had problems with intense, debilitating pain in his calf muscle compartments, often in games and occasionally in practices. Both the trainer and the physician indicated that the pain came when exercise caused the calf muscle (the gastrocnemius) to expand beyond the capacity of the muscle compartment. John had taken steroids in high school and had bulked up substantially. The calf muscles appeared to have expanded beyond the capacity of the muscle compartment. He was referred to me by his physician and the athletic trainer to help him ease the pain in those calf muscles when he exercised. The physician assured me that John would not damage the muscle by exercising it, even when it pressed against the compartment.

When he was not in a trance, John knew that the pain came after exercising the calf muscles. Even though he recognized that it didn't occur every time he exercised, he could not identify any discernible pattern to the onset of the pain. The pain rarely occurred in practices, but it occurred in football games and in intramural basketball games. Being a psychologist, I tend to look for psychological elements in problems. (Give a kid a hammer and everything needs hammering.)

John was interested in eliminating the pain and felt that hypnosis might be the solution. The coach had strongly urged that he work with me on this problem, as had the trainer. He was eager to try this and entered a trance rapidly after a short induction. Because the pain did not come each time he exercised the leg, I began by asking him what was going on when the pain started and what the pain meant to him. Little information on these questions had been forthcoming before John was in a trance, but in a trance much more information became available. He was able to recognize that the pain had something to do with making the all-conference team his freshman year. He had made all-state in both his junior and senior years in high school, and he had set out to make the all-conference team his freshman year of college. Somehow the calf muscle pain related to that all-conference goal. In several hypnosis sessions we went back to situations when he experienced the onset of the pain. We discovered that the pain came when he sensed someone else's performance was better than his. The pain in his calf muscles forced him to stop the exercise whenever he thought someone was outperforming him.

When it appeared that the pain was a way to get out of appearing second best, I made a posthypnotic suggestion that from then on his comparisons would be with his past performance rather than with any other person's performance. After the hypnosis sessions he followed this suggestion, and the occurrence of the pain rapidly disappeared.

The pain in his legs was a real pain with a genuine physical cause. Exercise did cause his calf muscles to enlarge and press on the compartment, but there was also an unsuspected psychological element that intensified the pain. The physical source of the pain was clear, but it took hypnosis to uncover the psychological element. When the psychological element was uncovered and eliminated, the physical element was diminished to an untroublesome level and thus the dis-ease eliminated.

CASE TWO: THE ASTHMATIC

Another university athlete was unable to participate fully in football practices because of asthma. He had suffered from this problem since junior high school days. In junior high and high school, he was large and strong enough to be the starter, even though his asthma kept him from participating full time in practice sessions. Now in the university, in spite of an impressive size and talent, he was the backup fullback because he was able to participate for only about half of each practice session. When his asthma kicked in he got choked up and clearly had to stop practicing. He had been to allergists who had found him allergic to a sizable array of commonly found factors. He kept the asthma somewhat under control with prescription inhalers, but these were not effective enough to allow him to practice fully.

Because his asthma never bothered him in games, and rarely bothered him outside of practices, I suspected a psychological element in the asthma. In a trance we went back to when the asthma started, which appeared to be in junior high school. This athlete loved the competitions, but thoroughly disliked football practices in junior high and high school. His outstanding size and talent made him see the practices as a waste of his energy. In junior high school and high school he was strong and talented enough to be the starting fullback, even though his asthma kept him out of a good share of each practice.

The asthma turned out to be closely related to his dislike of practice—an acceptable and effective way of being able to sit on the sidelines during practice, without keeping him from competing in the games. Again, this is an example of secondary gain. This was never a conscious process to him, but by the time he got to the university, getting choked up in football practice was firmly established, though unconscious.

Unfortunately for him, unlike high school where he was significantly better than any other fullback, in the university the competition was greater. Not being able to practice fully, he lost his starting position and was relegated to the backup position.

After the initial hypnosis session we discussed the causes of the asthma. He claimed that he did not dislike the university practices as he disliked practices in high school. In fact, he felt he gained much from participating in the university practices. He was rarely bored in the university practice sessions. At first he had trouble seeing that his attacks were not entirely caused by an allergy. However, he gradually seemed to accept this because, in the trance, getting choked up when he imaged being even a little bored in practice alerted him to this connection. The next problem was to help him overcome the asthma attacks.

We first worked on deep breathing. When he was not in a trance, I asked him to take a deep breath. At first he expanded his chest and sucked in his abdomen, but I worked with him on diaphragm breathing exercises until he could do this easily. Then we did some additional trance work. When he was in a trance, I had him image being in practice and being bored with the practice. Without my suggesting it, he felt some tightening in his chest. I made a suggestion that deep diaphragm breathing would open up the bronchial tubes any time he felt this tightening. When he took the deep breaths, he felt the tension ease. I made the suggestion that any time he felt a tightness, some deep breaths would open up these channels. Still in a trance I had him visualize this several times.

Then I asked him to image himself in a previous practice in which he had developed a full-blown attack. I allowed him to get choked up, but he was able to relieve it with deep breaths. The exercise was to make two things clear to him:

first, he had the ability to bring on an asthma attack with no allergy factor present, and second, he had a strategy for stopping the attack and releasing the bronchial tension. He ended our sessions with a good understanding of why he was having the attacks during practice and how he could eliminate them. I also gave him a suggestion, which he readily accepted, that he would enjoy his practices and would want to participate fully in them. This was actually a reinforcement because he did benefit from and enjoy the university practices.

Before our sessions he always took a powerful prescription inhaler with him to each practice. He would dope himself with it before practice and often during practice. The inhaler did not eliminate the attacks. At his first practice after we finished our sessions, he used his inhaler before practice, but found he could relieve any tightness with the deep breaths. At the second practice, he took his inhaler with him but did not use it before or during practice. After several practice sessions he realized he could control any tightness without the inhaler, and he found that he was having fewer occasions that needed the deep breathing. He found practices more enjoyable and soon regained his starting position with the team. (I had a small twinge of conscience about the other fullback who lost his starting position.)

Physical Injuries

Most athletic injuries do not have an underlying psychological cause. The strained muscles and bruises usually encountered in a training room have clearly physical origins. It is nonetheless possible to use hypnosis to help an athlete mobilize his or her inner resources to speed a recovery. In a trance, a subject can control some autonomic functions—functions that we do not usually consider consciously controllable.

PILOT STUDY OF HEALING

Hypnosis can help an athlete to mobilize these autonomic functions to aid in injury recovery. I conducted a pilot study with football players to investigate this use of hypnosis.

During the fall football season, I selected 10 players at random who had been injured severely enough to be out of practice and competition for at least two weeks. The athletes were selected for this experiment after the head trainer estimated their recovery times. The training room staff did not always know which athletes I worked with and, other than the hypnosis sessions, they received no special treatment by the training room staff.

Using hypnosis, I worked with each athlete individually for about one hour. I explained that within each of us is a Force for Health which takes care of any healing we need. This force knows how to make the skin grow back together after a cut, heal a strained muscle, and cure any diseases. We don't usually feel this force, but we can strengthen it and feel it. (This force and its manipulation are not generally recognized by Western medicine, but those familiar with Chinese medicine will recognize its similarity to Chi.)

While the athlete was in a trance, I asked him to inhale deeply several times. I suggested that as he inhaled, he would feel energy coming into his body and as he exhaled, he would feel this energy concentrating into a ball—probably in his abdomen but perhaps some other place in his body. He might feel this after one deep breath, but would certainly feel it after two deep breaths. When he felt this ball of energy, he nodded his head to let me know. Then I asked him to send this mobilized energy to the site of the injury. When the ball arrived at the injury, it would melt into the injured site. As this happened, the site would become free of pain and he would feel a slight tingling and a bit of comfortable warmth. These signs let him know that his healing force was working on the injury.

After practicing this several times, I suggested the athlete would do this at least three times per day—at night in bed, upon waking in the morning, some time around the middle of the day, and anytime he felt pain at the injury site. I suggested that the warmth and tingling are caused by an increased flow of curative fluids to the site.

After bringing the athlete out of the trance, I suggested that he take a couple deep breaths, feel the energy ball, and send it to the effected part. On the occasional times when the athlete could not bring on these feelings when out of the trance, I reinduced the trance and reinforced the suggestions. The second session almost always enabled the athlete to feel the Force for Health without being in a trance.

At the end of the football season, we compared the recovery times of the 10 athletes who had been hypnotized (the experimental group) with 20 others with comparable recovery estimates (the control group). We found that for the control group, the average of the trainer's estimates of recovery time was pretty much on target, while the average for the experimental group was clearly less than the estimated time. There were enough participants in the study to achieve a $p<.10$. (A $p<.10$ means there was less than 1 chance in 10 that the results were a chance variation, or 9 chances out of 10 that the hypnosis did speed the recovery time.) This significance is not enough for a publishable study, but it is enough to strongly suggest that hypnosis sessions made a substantial contribution to the rehabilitation of these athletic injuries. I hope to repeat this study in the future with more participants.

Controlling Blood Flow

Hunter (1987) showed how easy it is to demonstrate that a person can control blood flow in a trance. In demonstrations using the same technique, I sterilize the back of a person's hand. Then I hypnotically anesthetize the hand, pull up a flap of skin from the back of the hand, and insert a large sterile needle (usually a #20, 1 1/2-inch needle) through the flap. I suggest that the person will be able to open the eyes to look at the needle without coming out of the trance. With the needle inserted, I ask the person to choose whether the bleeding will take place on the hole toward the thumb or the hole away from the thumb when I remove the needle. There is no bleeding until I remove the needle, but when I do remove the needle, the chosen side will bleed and the other one will not bleed. Normal clotting will stop the bleeding in about 15 seconds, but during that time, the person can demonstrate allowing bleeding at either hole, both holes, or neither hole (see figure 11.1 on page 130).

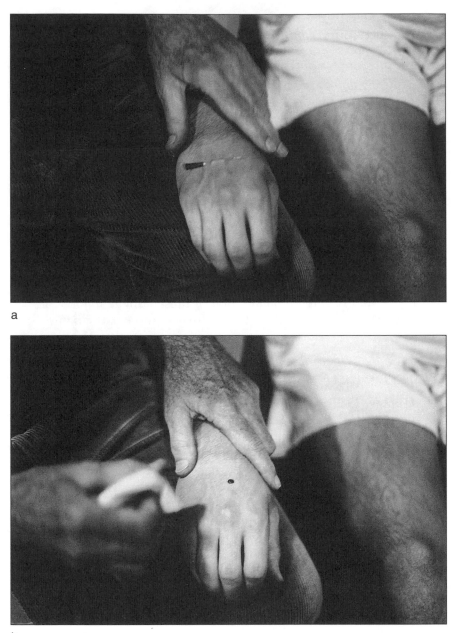

a

b

Figure 11.1   Controlling blood flow experiment with *(a)* inserting the sterile needle and *(b)* controlling the blood flow through one of the holes in the skin.

I do not understand how a person mobilizes these internal forces, but I have demonstrated to many athletes that they can do it. In one case I was baffled. I pulled the needle out, and there was no blood from either side. Then after about five seconds the bleeding started at the designated hole. During the time of no bleeding, I was sure that my demonstration was a failure. Later, when the subject was not in a trance, he asked me whether I knew why the bleeding did not start right away. I admitted being baffled. He explained that although he said he would allow bleeding on the thumb side, he had silently decided that he would not bleed for a bit on either side. As soon as he saw that he could stop both sides from bleeding, he allowed the bleeding to start on the selected side. Rather than being a failure, the demonstration showed not only that we can control bleeding, but also that a person in a trance still has an important degree of control.

The potential for using hypnosis to accelerate healing is rarely tapped in sports. I have found some trainers receptive to trying hypnosis, but some seem resistant. Perhaps this is caused by the lack of information about hypnosis in the training programs for athletic trainers. A fear of the unknown affects us all. Hypnosis is a force that should be more frequently and effectively used in healing.

LEARNING FROM CASE STUDIES

The individual skills that empower performance are discussed in part II. In practice, these skills are not usually isolated but are integrated into the mental training workout. Part III presents a variety of case studies that show how these skills are developed when working with individual athletes. They illustrate the ways in which hypnosis is effectively used to develop strong, mentally tough athletes.

WHAT'S THE WORST THING THAT CAN HAPPEN TO A
QUARTERBACK? HE LOSES HIS CONFIDENCE.

TERRY BRADSHAW, FOOTBALL QUARTERBACK

Chapter 12
David, the Quarterback

I start the case study section with David's case because it illustrates how hypnosis was able to enhance some of the usual techniques of sport psychology—arousal control, imagery, self-confidence, and optimism. David might have been able to achieve the changes in his performance with techniques familiar to most sport psychologists, but this case illustrates how he achieved them more quickly with hypnosis.

Adjusting to Bigger Games

I worked with David over a couple months, at first weekly, then about every other week. The early sessions were rarely more than half an hour, and later sessions only 15 minutes or less.

David had just graduated from high school and was taking a year off between high school and college. He had done well in high school football and was interested in qualifying for an athletic scholarship to play on a good university team and perhaps eventually for a pro team. I met him when he was just starting with a semipro team.

Semipro Football

Semipro teams practice on Tuesdays and Thursdays during late spring and summer, from 6:30 P.M. to 9 P.M. They schedule about 10 games on Saturday evenings between late June and early September. There are leagues for these teams, along with playoffs for district, regional, and national championships. Fund-raising activities and sponsors who advertise in the team programs pay for uniforms and playing fields. The players are not paid for practices or games, and they provide their own transportation to games whether at home or away. Because no one on these teams gets paid, we should emphasize the semi in the term semipro.

These teams consist of players who are not currently on any university or professional teams. Some have played on university teams, some on junior college teams, and others only for high school teams. Most are out just for the fun of playing quality football, but a few hope to hone their skills and be noticed by a professional team.

David's Problems

The coach asked me if I thought I could help David. The coach was familiar with David's work with his high school team and felt he could be a valuable team member. He sensed that David needed to be more relaxed—he was much too tense and nervous to perform well with the team. He was not showing the talent that he had when playing on his high school team. He recognized that David was much younger than most of the other players and that this age and experience difference was particularly critical for a quarterback—a player who must serve as a team leader.

The coach felt that David's tension was causing him to become confused on some of the plays and to throw less accurately than he had in high school. The coach had two other quarterbacks, but felt that David had the ability to develop into at least the second quarterback for the team.

When the coach suggested to David that I might help him in his confidence problems, David was eager to begin working with me as soon as possible. He was interested in anything that might help with his performance. He recognized that his anxiety interfered with his performance. This anxiety hadn't bothered him in high school or when he played with friends his age. At 19, he was younger, by far, than any other member of this semipro team. His prior experience was with teammates his age, and he was impressed, more accurately overawed, with the experience and maturity of these teammates, most of whom had played on university teams. David keenly felt his lack of experience.

I had noticed that in warm-up runs, David usually came in ahead of most older members of the team. It was clear that he was in much better physical condition than his older teammates. When I pointed this out to him, it helped him feel a little less cowed by them.

Arousal Control

As with most other athletes who feel hypnosis might help them, David proved to be highly hypnotizable. He was able to enter a trance rapidly and deeply.

My first step with David was to help him control his anxiety. I explain this procedure in chapter 7, "Optimizing Arousal Levels." Briefly, it consists of having David relive in a trance how he felt when he was playing well, with his body relaxed and under control and his mind focused on the game. The procedure I used taught him how to regain this composure by a couple deep breaths and some appropriate self-affirming statements. While in a trance, David was able to image himself bringing his arousal under control in several instances when he had been overaroused in practice sessions.

Self-Confidence

As far as I could tell by observing and by talking to other team members, they had no concern or resentment that David's only previous football experience was at a high school level. They seemed to accept him as one of the team, not recognizing how impressed David was by their size and experience or how this was affecting his playing ability. David, however, felt his lack of experience keenly and was, in my view, overly impressed with the older team members. The tenseness that the coach had noted seemed related to a lack of confidence. Because self-confidence seemed to be a continuing problem, in another session I used a form of the ego-strengthening script outlined in chapter 9. Sometimes I just read this script, inserting relevant references at points indicated in the script. David responded to this well, and I used shortened versions of the script numerous times during our work together.

Imaging Plays

A second step was to help him get the various plays under control. Most members of the team were veterans and knew all the plays from previous years, while David had to learn these plays on his own. There was no play book—the plays were described on the practice field and then run. He believed that he could fix the plays in his mind only by executing the plays on the practice field. He had a lot of trouble imagining himself executing the plays or learning from watching the other quarterbacks execute the plays. Because he was third in line for the quarterback position, he did not get many repetitions in practice sessions and, of course, no time in the games. At first I had some difficulty getting him to react kinesthetically when he imaged the plays. After some deepening and my suggesting that he fake feeling the muscles twitch as he imaged plays, he began to feel himself actually executing the plays while in a trance. The faking of the kinesthetic response was probably the most effective way to help him get the kinesthetic reaction when imaging. I have found that the kinesthetic reaction is important in fixing the plays mentally and physically. (See chapter 14, "Matt, the Kayaker," for more on establishing kinesthetic imagery.)

Self-Hypnosis

Because David needed to feel himself completing these plays multiple times, I decided that he could best do this on his own using self-hypnosis. Although David was responsive to hetero-hypnosis, it took some time for him to learn to self-induce a trance. Teaching self-hypnosis is described in chapter 1.

After I taught David self-hypnosis, I had him put himself into a trance and come out several times to establish this self-hypnosis ability. After he was able to comfortably self-induce a trance, I began to help him image the play formations he had to master in the self-induced trances.

We again had the same problem in getting a kinesthetic reaction when he imaged the plays in self-hypnosis. This was not unexpected because self-induced trances are usually not as deep as hetero-induced ones. After again suggesting that he fake the response, we began to get a kinesthetic reaction more automatically when he imaged the plays. After he had imaged several plays effectively, I suggested that between practices he put himself in a trance at home and go over each play several times.

The next week, he reported that he was able to do this. The imaging on his own seemed to get him at ease with the limited variety of formations that this team used.

Building Optimism

In talking to David about his playing, I suspected some problems with what Seligman termed optimism. Seligman has proposed that an optimistic outlook by an athlete is associated with faster learning and better performance. I gave David the test from Seligman's book, *Learned Optimism* (1990). The scores indicated that David dealt with his errors somewhat optimistically but with his successes rather pessimistically, and that overall, David's attitude was more pessimistic than optimistic. This meant that he attributed his bad events to external factors that were temporary and specific, but he also attributed his successes the same way. An athlete with an optimistic outlook attributes his successes to personal efforts and to pervasive and permanent favorable factors in the environment. Success provides a reinforcement for the attributions which the athlete uses to explain the success. If the athlete attributes the success to the athlete's own efforts and skills, these efforts and skills are reinforced. If the athlete attributes the success to external and temporary factors, the athlete is not appropriately reinforced by the successes. This seemed to be David's problem.

The test results led to some extended conversations in which we talked about what he considered the reasons for his successes. His statements confirmed the results of the Seligman test. When he thought about the practices that had gone well, he attributed it to a good feel of the ball. "That day the ball just seemed to fit into my hand and go just where I wanted it to go." Clearly he was attributing his success to factors that were external, temporary, and specific. I helped David recognize these as nonhelpful attributions, and we worked on personal attributions that would allow him to take personal credit for doing well. There were some reasons that the ball fit well into his hand. His success was caused by his practicing regularly, staying alert, feeling confident, and otherwise because of his own skills and effort. Repeating these attributions helped him to sustain a quality performance and to retain this good feeling. He began to see good performance as something more within his control—not caused by external factors such as the way the ball felt.

He was able to deal with his less successful sessions well. One evening when he had not done as well as usual, I talked to him after practice. He noted that in the practice the offense and defense had worn the same color jerseys, and he could not always immediately separate the receivers from the defenders—a temporary, external, specific attribution for the error problem. Although he attributed some of the problem to external factors, he was also able to see problems with his actions. He seemed able to gain some lessons from the less successful sessions and not let the problems get him down.

The A B C D Es of Ellis were helpful in getting more positive attributions for success. In the case of his successful evenings, the Activation, we were able to Dispute the temporary and external nature of the Belief that it was the ball that caused the success (the Condition), and Energize a belief that David was responsible for the success and that he could repeat it at other practices.

We continued the discussions of his attributions, sometimes in a trance and sometimes not. The attributions he gave for his successes became more permanent, pervasive, and personal. His analyses of his successes were realistic and helpful, and he could similarly look at his failures as learning experiences.

Therapy Results

During the course of our sessions, David said that the most important difference was his gain in self-confidence. The ability to visualize and practice the plays on his own contributed to this confidence. He also felt the ability to analyze accurately the factors that affected his successes and failures in practice sessions was a major source of his improvement. He found that he was much more in control of his performance than he had been in high school.

The coach reported a steady improvement in David's performance. By the end of the season, he felt that David was playing on a par with the more experienced quarterbacks, and he scheduled David for playing time. He told me that he was sure David would be the starting quarterback for at least some games next season.

As mentioned at the start of this case, much of David's problem could be helped by standard sport psychology techniques. David felt that self-hypnosis for rehearsing plays was "really cool," which I assume meant helpful. I believe that hypnosis helped me to detect and focus on the significant aspects of David's mental problems and thus alleviate them in much less time than would have been possible without hypnosis. David enthusiastically agrees with this claim.

SOMETIMES YOU DON'T KNOW YOU CAN DO IT UNTIL YOU TRY.

MICHELLE AKERS, WORLD CHAMPION SOCCER PLAYER

CHAPTER 13
SCOTT, THE SOCCER PLAYER

This case study was written jointly by Bud Lewis, Wilmington College's soccer coach, and me. It sets out the sequence of events that led to a remarkable healing. It shows how we can use the techniques of relaxation and imagery to mobilize the healing powers inherent in any person. It also presents a coach's reaction to his first exposure to the use of hypnosis.

Coach Lewis' Story

To me it was a transformation bordering on the miraculous. An athlete who for two years had been severely restricted by a painful hamstring was almost instantly relieved of this pain by a procedure I had not imagined possible.

As a former collegiate and professional player and as the men's head soccer coach at Wilmington College (Ohio) for the past 20 years, I have seen or experienced numerous injuries, rehab techniques, and procedures. I have had considerable training and education in the care and prevention of athletic-related injuries. However, never in my playing and coaching experiences had I observed an athlete's healing, pain reduction, and flexibility increase as a result of hypnotherapy.

Scott Harting, a first-year player from Dayton, Ohio, experienced considerable pain and discomfort midway through our 1994 fall season as a result of chronic tight hamstrings. Scott was 6 feet 2 inches tall and weighed 185 pounds. When recruiting Scott to Wilmington College the previous year, I observed one of his high school games in which his playing time was severely limited by a pulled right hamstring. During the 15 minutes he played, he scored two goals, including the game winner. His high school coach assured me that if we could keep him healthy, he would make an outstanding college player.

Five weeks into the fall soccer season of his high school senior year (1993), Scott first experienced hamstring problems. He immediately began treatment at St. Elizabeth Medical Hospital (Dayton) in their Sports Rehab and Physical Therapy Center. For the five weeks remaining in his season, Scott attended two rehab sessions per week. His therapy included ultrasound stimulus, electro-muscular stimulus (EMS), massage, and assisted stretching. Each rehab session lasted a little over an hour and was painful. Although Scott experienced temporary relief and improved flexibility, his pain and discomfort returned within hours of the treatment.

Following his fall season, Scott took a hiatus from playing soccer during all of November and December 1993 and January and most of February 1994. While playing club ball in late March, he experienced a severe muscle strain of his left hamstring, similar to the previous right hamstring injury. Scott resumed playing soccer later that spring and through the summer and experienced less discomfort in warmer weather.

With the Wilmington College men's soccer team (fall 1994), Scott's first month of training and games was uneventful in relation to hamstring problems. During this time our athletic trainers were providing constant care and attention to improve his hamstring flexibility by using a rigorous stretching program. For as long as Scott could remember, he was never able to touch his toes while bending at the waist. Midshin was the farthest he could reach when he attempted to touch his toes with his legs together and no bending at the knees.

As the weather became colder, Scott began experiencing considerable hamstring pain and was seldom able to train for any length of time. Early in the fall, he was getting 30 to 45 minutes of playing time per game. However, by early October he was asking to come out of matches after only 10 or 15 minutes because of the extreme pain he was experiencing. Our athletic trainers indicated that Scott was religious about getting his rehab therapy once or twice a day, which included EMS and assisted stretching. Scott took a week off from playing and training, but the pain returned immediately upon resuming training with the team. At this point Scott was seriously contemplating leaving the game. The chronic pain and resulting frustration for the past year was having a toll on his usually optimistic outlook.

During the third week of October 1994, when checking our trainers' list of players with practice restrictions caused by injuries, I noticed that Scott was scheduled to see a doctor. I was pleased that he was looking for additional diagnosis and possibly new treatment for his hamstrings. During our afternoon training, Scott returned from his doctor's appointment and, along with his trainer, immediately came over to me. He said, "Coach, I can touch my toes, and the pain in my hamstring is almost gone!" He proceeded to touch his toes, *grab his toes*, and the look in his eyes and his expression was pure joy. Scott was ecstatic, and I was astounded.

I questioned him about his treatment, and he told me he had been hypnotized by Dr. Donald Liggett. I had assumed that Scott was going to an MD rather than a PhD. I had known Don when he was a professor of psychology at Wilmington College but I had not heard that he was in town visiting friends and had stopped to see faculty and students in the athletic trainers' office that day.

Therapist's Diagnosis

During my visit to Wilmington, I stopped by the training room to visit former colleagues. The trainer, with whom I had worked when I was an active faculty member, talked to me about Scott's pain and lack of flexibility. I was not told about all the previous treatment he had received. Because the trainer knew that I had previously helped other athletes with flexibility problems, he asked me if I could help Scott. (For an earlier example of increasing flexibility, see Liggett & Hamada, 1993.)

I met with Scott when he came in for treatment after Wednesday's practice. The trainer had told me that Scott came in regularly for his therapy and seemed to have no psychological or physical problems except the hamstring problem. When I talked to Scott, I could not detect any psychological problems. He seemed normally healthy, both physically and psychologically—an outgoing, active college student with some tight, painful hamstrings.

When Scott was seated comfortably, his calf and arm muscles felt relaxed, while his hamstrings felt contracted, noticeably more hard. I proceeded on the theory that the tenseness and the pain in the muscle were interrelated.

Typically, when a muscle is in pain, the body, as a reflex, tenses that muscle, which increases the pain. This additional pain causes more tenseness, thus more pain, and a cycle of pain and tension is established. The individual can often interrupt this cycle by reducing either the tension or the pain. Hypnosis can be effective in reducing both of these. One useful characteristic of hypnosis is its ability to relax the subject. Anyone in a trance is usually less tensed than when out of a trance. In addition to this relaxation, you can give suggestions in a trance for further relaxation, and these suggestions will carry over, at least for a time, when the subject is out of the trance.

To a person in a trance, suggestions of anesthesia for a part of the body are also effective. Pain control is a long-established contribution of hypnosis. (E.R. & J.R. Hilgard's 1975 book *Hypnosis in the Relief of Pain* is a standard work on hypnosis.) There are some important cautions in pain control, however. Pain is usually a signal to the body that something is wrong, and we should not erase pain signals willy-nilly. Before eliminating pain, a therapist should always investigate the cause of the pain and its useful function. In Scott's case, the trainer and the physician had indicated that he was unlikely to injure his hamstring further by playing soccer or stretching exercises, so pain relief seemed appropriate.

Therapy

Scott was not sure what to think about treating his problem with hypnosis. Although he was not at all optimistic about the effectiveness of hypnosis, he was most eager for help and thus open to any idea that had any chance of improving his condition.

At the beginning of our first session, before attempting hypnosis, I asked Scott to stand up, bend over, and touch his toes. He could bring his fingertips only to about the middle of his shins. "It's the pain in my hamstrings that keeps me from going any farther." This was consistent with the previously mentioned tenseness in his hamstrings.

I used a progressive relaxation induction and some deepening. (Refer to the VMBR script, chapter 3.) One deepening technique I use is to bring a person in and out of the trance several times. After the first induction, Scott was able to respond almost instantly to a signal for reinduction and was able to enter a deep trance easily and rapidly. The only tests of susceptibility and trance depth that I normally use are the subjective impression of the subject and testing whether an arm rigidity suggestion holds when the person comes out of a trance. In Scott's case, both tests indicated a moderately deep level of trance. Scott's initial hypnosis itself relaxed all the muscles of his body, but I gave him additional suggestions to relax the hamstring muscles more completely.

While he was in a trance, I probed for any secondary gain associated with the hamstring pain. Secondary gain is a benefit, usually unconsciously realized, associated with suffering from a problem. Secondary gain—sympathy, attention, being excused from activity—is often enough to sustain a severe problem. I found no suggestion of this in Scott.

I used a technique with Scott that I have often found helpful to injured athletes. After achieving a reasonable depth of trance, I have the subject focus on a spot in his lower abdomen that I call the Center, or Force for Health. I had been using the idea of a Force for Health for several years before I was exposed to Bill Moyers' work with Chinese medicine in his TV series and book entitled *Healing and the Mind* (1993). It appears that this force has some similarities to what the Chinese call Chi or Qi, a concept more fully explained in David Eisenberg's (1985) *Encounters With Qi*. When in a trance, I ask the subject to focus on and feel this force by taking several deep abdominal breaths. I then suggest that the force will feel like a pleasant, vibrant ball of energy, probably in the lower abdomen, but perhaps somewhere else. If the subject does not know how to do abdominal breathing, that is, to use the diaphragm in deep breathing, I teach abdominal breathing before the subject goes into the trance.

When I used this procedure with Scott, he was able to feel this force after taking a couple deep breaths. When he sensed the force, I asked him to direct it to one of his hamstrings. As soon as he moved the force to the hamstring, he would feel a deeper relaxation in that muscle. It would feel slightly warm, maybe with a tingling sensation, and any hamstring pain would greatly ease. While in a trance, he realized all these sensations. I then instructed him to repeat this for his other hamstring, and he felt these sensations there too. In addition to easing the pain and relaxing the muscles, I told him that this force would know how to work on curing whatever was wrong with the muscle, and the force would do this whenever he directed it to the muscle. I suggested that anytime he wanted to, he would be able to take two deep abdominal breaths, feel the force, and send it to his hamstrings to ease any tenseness or pain he might be experiencing in those muscles. I suggested that he do this at least twice a day, whether or not he was feeling pain, to speed up any healing that those muscles needed.

This first session took about one hour. At the end of the session, Scott seemed pleased that his hamstrings felt distinctly different from the beginning of the session—the usual tenseness and pain were gone. When he bent over to touch his fingertips to the floor, he was delighted to find that he was easily able to touch the top of the toe of his shoe with no hamstring pain or tenseness. "I can't remember when I have ever been able to do this!" When he was seated, I felt his hamstring muscles, and the tightness that I felt at the beginning of the session was markedly reduced.

I asked Scott to come in again before the next afternoon practice for about half an hour to reinforce the suggestions from the first session. At that session, he told me that on his own after the first session he was able to elicit the force and had successfully transferred it to create the warmth, relaxation, and tingling in his hamstrings. I reinduced a trance and had him elicit the force with his deep breaths and send it to his hamstrings and feel the warmth, tingling, and pain relief. The only modification in suggestions from the first session was that when he called on the force, he could send it to both his hamstrings at once, rather than one at a time. At the end of the second session he had gained more flexibility, being able to touch his knuckles to the floor with no hamstring strain or pain. He was excited that he was able to put his fingers under his toes without bending his knees. He commented that his hamstrings felt even more relaxed and flexible than after the first session, and when I felt them, this seemed to be true. It was after this session that he went out to practice and grabbed his toes for Coach Lewis.

As a sidelight, occasionally an athlete with a similar problem will be offended by my offer to use hypnosis, interpreting the offer as my suggesting that the problem is psychological, that I think the problem is in his or her head, that it is not real. In such a case, I assure the athlete that I believe the problem, in a physiological sense, is not in his or her head. I explain the tension and pain cycle, and that the problem is much more likely a reflex reaction originating at some nerve center below the thinking brain. Using hypnosis, I can help the mind break the pain and tension cycle, that is, to begin to control that nervous reaction, and thus the muscles' behavior in a way that was not possible before. I think this is, in fact, what I was able to do with Scott's muscle problem. Some therapists would explain the problem in terms of the conscious and unconscious, but I have found my explanation coherent and certainly more acceptable.

Coach's Conclusion

Scott's sessions with Don Liggett produced an immediate and substantial physical change that I found amazing. Never had I seen so rapid a change in flexibility and reduction in a player's pain without medication or drugs. In the Thursday afternoon practice, after the second session with Dr. Liggett, Scott was able to fully participate in the team's training session for the first time in weeks. The next day he played, full go, without restrictions or pain, in a regular intercollegiate match. (In fact, Scott had an excellent game, scoring once and assisting on another goal.)

Questions about the long-term effects of the hypnosis and Scott's improved flexibility were in the back of all our minds. However, I am pleased to note that he successfully finished the fall season without any problems relating to his hamstrings. He had no problem in our spring season training and conditioning, which began in late February 1995, and throughout his college career he maintained excellent flexibility. Scott has not experienced any significant pain in his hamstrings and still once in a while delightedly grabs his toes for anyone willing to watch.

I have had the opportunity to observe numerous hypnotist entertainers. These hypnotists design their performances to display their genius at the expense of those hypnotized, and I had often wondered whether the power of hypnotism could perhaps be used to benefit, rather than to embarrass, the people hypnotized. I had not experienced the constructive uses of hypnotism until exposure to Dr. Liggett's work. He enlightened me to how hypnotism can help harness the tremendous ability of a willing participant's mind—to focus, create imagery, and produce bodily responses that can help improve an athlete's attitude, health, and performance.

Observing Scott's results from hypnosis was nothing short of amazing. Scott, along with trainers and the soccer team, were extremely thankful and excited about the results of this hypnosis procedure. Unfortunately for our soccer program, Dr. Liggett no longer resides in Ohio. Because of this experience with Scott and my other experiences observing the results of hypnosis, I am excited and confident about the use and application of hypnosis for athletes and nonathletes alike to improve flexibility and reduce the resulting pain. I would strongly urge athletes, coaches, athletic trainers, physicians, and others to take a serious look at the many possibilities offered by hypnosis in the care, treatment, and prevention of injuries.

Therapist's Postscript

This case illustrates how combining pain relief and relaxation can ease a long-standing problem quickly. Both relaxation and pain relief are in the repertoire of any competent hypnotherapist. Playing a minor role in this case were elements of imagery and self-confidence. Scott's long experience with the debilitating pain had contributed to a nonclinical depression and pessimism. The flexibility gain in itself did much to immediately instill a more optimistic outlook. The coach, trainer, and teammates recognized a changed personality when the pain was alleviated.

Using hypnosis with athletes is not nearly as extensive or well documented as in medicine or psychotherapy. Within the sports world, as elsewhere, there is still reluctance to consider its use. In this case, Scott suffered from the hamstring pain for more than a year. This was attributable to a lack of information about the potential of hypnosis and perhaps to the unavailability of a competent hypnotist.

Not all disabilities can be eased as effectively and rapidly as this one, and I was almost as surprised at the success as the trainer and the coach were. However, the immediate relief Scott gained and sustained throughout his college career helped to establish hypnosis as a valuable and viable treatment for the staff and athletes of this college.

Recently, when I checked with Scott on his hamstrings and to get his permission to use his name in this book, he reported, "I haven't had any major pain since meeting with you five years ago. My hamstrings are doing fine."

To add a personal note, nothing I have ever learned has enabled me to help others as much as hypnosis has. When someone like Scott escapes from an onerous debility, I get a lift which is hard to describe—I am on a cloud for days. Even after five years, when Scott reports his hamstrings are doing fine, I still feel this exhilaration.

ALL GREAT CHANGES ARE IRKSOME TO THE HUMAN
MIND.

JOHN ADAMS, U.S. PRESIDENT 1797–1801

CHAPTER 14
MATT, THE KAYAKER

Matt Lutz is the U.S. national champion wild-water kayaker. He has represented the United States in International World Cup and World Championship competitions for several years. Matt wanted help in modifying his stroke and improving his focus and anxiety during competitions. We worked together on these goals many times over several months. A more extended description of my work with Matt is in an article we wrote for the U.S. Canoe and Kayak Team magazine (Lutz & Liggett, 1998).

Changing the Stroke

We first worked to help him effect a change in his technique—a modification designed to get more power into his stroke. One aspect involved putting the paddle into the water at a slightly different angle. The other part of the change required a major alteration in the way he thought about and felt his stroke. The old way was to put the paddle in the water and pull it back along the side of the boat. The new way asked him to think of putting the paddle in the water, regarding it as fixed, and pulling himself and the kayak past the paddle.

When we are paddling a canoe or a kayak, most of us feel we are bringing the paddle alongside the boat. Putting the paddle in the water, feeling that the paddle is fixed, and pulling the body and the kayak forward past the paddle is a major shift in focus. As described in chapter 5, "Mobilizing Energy," if the change increased his power, he should feel a difference in the muscles of his body—perhaps feeling the force coming all the way from his toes to the paddle.

External Versus Internal Imagery

Sometimes when an athlete first images a performance, all he achieves is external imagery—the activity is seen as though viewed by a third person. The suggestions for a kinesthetic reaction meet with a blank wall.

Matt Lutz had this problem when we started working together. Matt proved susceptible to hypnosis, but for a while his imagery was entirely external with no kinesthetic reaction at all.

Sometimes, when an athlete wants to learn a new technique, it is useful to image someone else executing a perfect performance. After external imagery of a new technique, however, internal imagery is necessary to teach the body the technique. This rehearsal happens only in internal kinesthetic imagery.

Most athletes I work with have a much easier time realizing internal imagery than did Matt. Because Matt had such trouble with internal imagery, I describe our experience to illustrate a variety of techniques for establishing internal imagery—not because his experience was typical! His resistance to internal imagery was far from typical.

Methods of Generating Kinesthetic Reactions

I have found several ways to help an athlete who is having trouble imaging internally. Most athletes can experience internal imagery readily, but some require extensive assistance.

Deepening the Trance

The first way to stimulate kinesthetic imagery is to increase the trance depth, which can be done several ways. Fractionation is one way. This involves helping a person in and out of a trance several times. I used this with Matt, but it did not facilitate his internal imagery.

Then I had Matt image himself in a pleasant place and had him use as many senses as possible while in this place. After he imaged being in a pleasant place, which for him was an ocean beach, I had him feel the sun on his face or back, see a bird floating on the wind, listen to the wind in the trees, feel the sand between the toes of his bare feet, and smell the fresh air from the sea. Asking a person in a trance to use many different senses usually deepens the trance. With both the fractionation and the sensory enhancement, Matt felt he got deeper.

In my experience with athletes, one or both of these techniques usually allows the person to be deep enough to image internally. Although Matt did feel a deeper trance, neither of these resulted in a kinesthetic reaction when we again tried having him image his kayak stroke.

Imaging Strenuous Activity

Another method of achieving the internal imagery is having the athlete image some particularly strenuous activity. If the athlete is familiar with bench pressing, that is an easy one to use. I knew that Matt worked out with weights, so I helped him into a trance again and suggested we go to the gym and lift weights. He felt himself lying on the bench. I used his kayak paddle as a bar for bench pressing. A prop like this can help in developing the imagery. I had him decide on a heavy weight to lift, and I provided some resistance to the bar as he lifted. My pressure was much less than he was imaging, and I gradually lightened my pressure as he completed several sets of repetitions, imaging increasing weights. Soon he was visualizing a heavy lift with little pressure from me. When he was out of the trance he was surprised that I had not been pushing down on the bar heavily. This exercise gave him the experience of internal imagery, and he was able then to get a kinesthetic reaction with his imagery of paddling.

Imaging the Kayaking

When he was finally able to internally image his kayak run, we first imaged the run he had made at the World Championships in Garmisch, Germany. He clearly saw the course, felt the water, the strokes, and the thrill of the competition. Then we started to work on the new stroke. The imagery of using the new stroke went well after he achieved the internal imagery. Matt knew exactly how he was supposed to do the new stroke. He had been able to do it in the water, but not consistently. He imaged the stroke in slow motion at first until it felt natural to him. Then we gradually sped up the stroke, being sure to maintain the proper form, until he was paddling at the speed he would be using in the water. He said the sessions proved to him that there was definitely an advantage to hypnotic visualizations. His recall of the run at Garmisch was thoroughly real. Afterward he said, "Never before had I experienced such muscular reaction during visualization as I did in those sessions, particularly when working on the new stroke. My body felt that it was actually paddling down the course at Garmisch. My stomach was tight, my back was gorged with blood, and my arms were full of acid. Hypnotic visualization was definitely my edge" (Lutz & Liggett, 1998 p. 7).

The changes had a major effect on the balance Matt felt because more of his entire body force was on the paddle. Because this technique increased the force on the paddle, the time the paddle was in the water was shorter, and there was a significant change in the stroke's rhythm—first the catch (when the paddle enters the water), the power stroke, the flip out of the water, the quick recovery, then the catch on the other side, and so on. For an experienced athlete with a well-established pattern, making such a major change in technique is difficult.

In the hypnotic session, he was able to image these changes. He had been trying to make this change in his own imagery, that is, without hypnosis, but was not able to get much kinesthetic reaction (internal imagery). He always reverted to the old technique when he got back on the water.

When we worked together to image the new technique in a trance, he was able to practice the new technique slowly, gradually increasing it to full speed. His imagery felt real to him.

After practicing this imagery several times at real-life speed in a trance, he found he could transfer this technique to the water easily. The rhythm he had imaged became automatic in the water.

Matt found imagery in hypnosis enabled him to focus on the energy bursts, bring his muscles more fully into the action, and change the pattern of his technique. He made the power stroke on the out breath and inhaled between the strokes to maximize the efficiency of his energy use.

The role of the sport psychologist in these instances is not to suggest new techniques to the athlete (that is the role of the coach), but to help the athlete see and feel the effect of the changed technique. While working in this area, as in other areas, it is vital that the psychologist work closely with the coach when making technique changes.

Teaching Self-Hypnosis

As I do with many athletes, I taught Matt how to put himself into a trance so he could image the new stroke on his own. He was able to do this, though he said the imagery with self-hypnosis was not as real as with hetero-hypnosis. In some additional sessions we worked on getting deeper into a self-induced trance. After several sessions he was able to get deeper, but was never able to get as deep, to get as real a sensation, as in hetero-hypnosis. This lesser intensity in self-hypnosis is not unusual. Repetitions in his own trance, however, were still helpful in teaching his body to master the new stroke.

After using imagery in our sessions and on his own, he found that using the new stroke in the water was almost natural to him. He was soon doing the new stroke without much thought about it. The hypnotic imagery was an effective method of teaching his body this new stroke.

Usually helping an athlete with internal imagery is not this difficult. Many are able to do it as soon as you ask them to feel the muscular reaction in the imagery. However, having a variety of techniques for helping an athlete learn to do internal imagery is sometimes necessary.

Focus and Concentration

One area Matt needed to work on was his self-talk before and during a competition. As Matt described his thoughts and actions, it seemed clear that some of his self-talk was destructive of good performance in the race. I used the muscle-testing demonstration of the effect of self-talk described in chapter 9, "Gaining Inner Strength." He could feel his strength increase as he changed from saying, "I hope," to saying, "I'll try," to, "I will." I also demonstrated how his strength decreased when he worried about the problems of the run compared with thinking of how successfully he would make the run. We worked on constructive self-talk for before the race—reminding himself how well he knew the course, how prepared he was, how much he would enjoy the excitement of the competitions, and other positive statements. These would take the place of concerns about tough spots in the course and other anxiety-producing thoughts.

When he described his thoughts as he ran the Garmish course, I noted many comments about the rocks. Although this may seem appropriate, it is more productive to focus on the line that the kayak must take. I suggested that he focus his attention on the line that he was to take through the water, rather than thinking of the rocks. Of course the rocks determine the line, but his focus should be the line and not the rocks. As in many aspects of life, what you focus on is what you get. Focus on the rocks, hit the rocks—focus on the line, hit the line.

Concentrating on the line was so logical that Matt wondered why he hadn't been thinking of this earlier. We visualized several runs in which he focused on the line. As he changed to this focus, he found that he could follow a much straighter path through the water. Less maneuvering was necessary, and this cut down the time for the run. After changing the focus from the rocks to the line, we began to focus on the line farther and farther ahead of the kayak.

Therapy Results

Matt felt a definite lift in self-confidence in his practices and in the competitions. He was down in bed for four days with a sinus infection 10 days before the May 1998 World Championships. He could not practice on the run as he normally would have done. While in bed, however, he used his self-hypnosis to image the run. He said that if not for the confidence instilled in him from the hypnosis sessions, he surely would have given up long before the race. Though still not back to his full strength from the four days of enforced idleness, he felt strong and confident on the race day. He finished 38th overall, up from his 44th place finish in the 1996 competition.

The World Cup Circuit, which took place at various European locations in June and July 1998, went even better than the May World Championships and his 1996 World Cups. He had placings at 28th, up from his placings in the 40s at the 1996 World Cups. In both the World Cups and the World Championships, his were the best American finishes.

Matt is now looking forward to the 2000 Championships, using imagery to learn the course. The World Championships will be the first race after 1998, and he has planned that a few more sessions with me will be an integral part of his preparation.

SOONER OR LATER YOU ACT OUT WHAT YOU THINK.
WHAT YOU THINK IS WHAT YOU'LL GET.
DR. BEE EPSTEIN-SHEPARD, SPORT PSYCHOLOGIST

CHAPTER 15
JIM, THE POLE-VAULTER

The university track coach asked me if I could help Jim. The coach was concerned that Jim was never able to do as well in a meet as he did in practice. He thought the problem had a psychological basis and that I might help. Jim seemed eager to work with me because he also felt that some psychological factor was involved with his problem of performing well in meets.

Losing the Edge

When I talked to Jim about his performance problem, he said he didn't feel nervous in the meets but always seemed to lose his edge and he didn't know why. He said he had been doing poorly in meets for so long that he and everybody else expected it. Though he was discouraged, he believed that a psychologist could help him find a key to his problem.

I expected Jim to be easily hypnotized so I used Spiegel's eye-roll induction (described in Spiegel & Spiegel, 1978). I use this induction frequently because it is faster than a progressive relaxation induction, and I can supplement it by progressive relaxation if the participant does not easily enter a trance. Probably because Jim was well motivated for help, he entered a trance easily.

Imaging a Good Vault

While in the trance I suggested that Jim visualize himself in a practice session when he was vaulting well, with good form, and achieving good heights. I asked him to picture himself at the end of the runway and to tell me how his body and mind felt. He gave the words, "calm, strong, focused, and confident." I grasped his elbow firmly to anchor these feelings. I expected to use the technique described in chapter 7, "Optimizing Arousal Levels."

Imaging the Last Meet

I asked him to go to the last meet, in which his best vault was about 16 inches below his best in practice. When he visualized himself at the end of the runway he felt unsure, concerned, and exposed. He said he was uncomfortably aware of many people watching him. He knew his coach and teammates were watching him knowing he would miss the vault. I had expected the usual feeling of excess arousal and tenseness, which is often the problem with diminished performance in competitions. Jim's problem seemed different. Although performance arousal is usually an important factor in performance, in Jim's case it seemed his lack of confidence was more debilitating than an inappropriate arousal level, and this lack of confidence was connected to what he thought his coach and teammates were thinking. What they were actually thinking, of course, is much less significant than what Jim imagined they were thinking. Perceptions control us more than does reality. I might have detected that Jim did not have the typical arousal problem when he told me early in our conversation that he didn't feel nervous in the meets.

I had Jim continue to image himself at the meet, at the end of the runway. I suggested that as he inhaled a deep breath, he would say, "focus," and he would be aware of only the runway and the open space above the bar. (Note: think of the bar, hit the bar; think of the open space above the bar, hit the open space.) He would feel as unobserved as he had in practice. As he exhaled he would say, "calm," and he would feel as he did in practice. I grasped his elbow to anchor the good feelings. We imaged several vaults using these cues.

Securing the Coach's Help

Before the next practice, I took the coach aside and told him of Jim's perception of the coach's expectation (or lack of expectation). The coach admitted he wondered if Jim would continue to miss his vaults at the meets, but he didn't realize he had conveyed these feelings to Jim. I added that I was sure he hadn't intended to convey this lack of confidence, but Jim had picked it up, and it was affecting his confidence. The coach's response was most positive. He said he would clearly but not too obviously express more confidence to Jim, in practice and at the meets. He thought he could easily do this in connection with my working with Jim. Several of his teammates also told him how I had helped them and how they were sure my help would eliminate his problem. They said they looked forward to seeing Jim out of the problem at the next meet.

Suggesting Appropriate Self-Talk

In our next session, I used the muscle-testing exercise with Jim (see chapter 9). I tested his strength as he thought of the coach and teammates doubting he could vault well. Then I asked him to think of their support and tested his strength again. The difference in the arm strength was clear to him. I suggested he should assure himself the coach and teammates were supporting him whether or not they were. He said he wouldn't have to pretend—the coach and the teammates knew, after working with me, he would get a new personal best at the next meet. He said that they told him that my work with him would get him out of his problem. (I hoped this would do as much for his confidence as it did for mine!) As he imaged himself at the next meet, he clearly felt their support. I asked him how high he would be vaulting at that meet, and he indicated his best height in practice. He imaged easily clearing that height. He had definitely internalized the confidence that his coach and teammates had expressed to him. When I brought him out of the trance, he was sure that he would get a new personal best at his next meet.

Imaging a Trampoline

At this second session he said he had some problems with his takeoff. He was not getting as much lift as he felt he should. Jim had been a diver in high school and knew the lift a trampoline provides. I suggested that when he took off for the vault he would feel this lift. (This is an example of the imaging discussed in chapter 4, "Imaging Perfect Performance.") He imaged a few vaults feeling this special lift as he took off for each vault. I suggested he would feel this lift whenever he vaulted. He later tried this imagery in practice and reported he could feel the difference.

Setting Goals

In our next session we worked on developing targets for practice and for the upcoming meets. Again in a trance, he decided he could increase his height by four inches in practice sessions during the two weeks before the next important meet. I asked him how he would feel when he achieved this increase, to establish memories of his future. We spent time visualizing how he would feel and how others would react to the improvement. He mentioned how happy the coach would be; then he mentioned how pleased his girlfriend would be. Interestingly, this was the first time he mentioned his girlfriend in our sessions. Out of curiosity I asked him what sort of vibes he got from his girlfriend at the meets. Did she doubt his performance at the meets too? He laughed and denied this vigorously. He said she was the only one who believed he would do well in meets, but, he added, she definitely didn't know as much about pole-vaulting as his coach and teammates! (An interesting example of dismissing possible support.)

Therapy Results

During the next week, he achieved his four-inch gain, and he set another target of two more inches for the week before the meet. Again we imaged the good feelings that would come from these memories of the future.

On our last session before the meet, we imaged his vaults at the new heights he achieved in practice. He felt the lift from the trampoline, and he felt the approval of his coach, teammates, and now we added the girlfriend.

The next meet was a great success. Shortly before his event, the coach assured Jim he knew my work with Jim would enable him to beat his best practice height, and he received similar comments from some teammates about his recent gains in practice. His confidence was soaring. He reported that as he took his two deep breaths at the end of the runway he became tightly focused, strong, and calm. He knew his coach and his teammates were watching him, knowing he would turn in his best performance ever. He even felt the trampoline as he took off. He beat his best practice vault by two inches and incidentally won the event with this new personal best.

Concluding Comment

This case helped me realize that arousal control is not the answer to every performance problem. Often in a trance an athlete will reveal different performance problems. In Jim's case it was a contagious expectation of failure and a feeling of lack of support rather than inappropriate arousal. These feelings were not expressed in our pretrance conversations but became clear as he imaged his feelings in a trance. The solution involved working with the coach, who easily and cooperatively understood and accepted his part in the problem and in the solution. Being open to possibilities, rather than deciding on the nature of a problem ahead of time, is an essential part of good therapy.

HYPNOSIS REPRESENTS A CAPACITY TO CONCENTRATE
ATTENTION AND TO RESIST DISTRACTIONS.

E.R. HILGARD, AMERICAN PSYCHOLOGIST

CHAPTER 16
BETH, THE BASKETBALL PLAYER

Beth, a college basketball player, wanted to boost her free throw percentage. She was just starting her senior season. In her junior year, she made only 42 percent of her free throws, and that was not enough to keep her or her coach happy. Beth dreaded stepping up to the free throw line. Her confidence was nil. She thought the problem might have a mental component and asked for my help.

Making Free Throws

Any basketball player good enough to get on a collegiate or professional team is skilled enough to make almost 100 percent of her free throws. They are called free throws because they are easy to make. A player whose percentage is less than 95 has mental problems—not psychiatric problems, but problems of focus and concentration. I have found that simple work with hypnosis can help most players eliminate the debilitating distractions ($P = C - D$, Performance equals Capability minus Distractions) and bring their free throw performance above 90 percent.

At least two factors cause the problems. The first is the change of focus required for a free throw. In the game situation a good player stays aware of the position of all her teammates and the opposing players. This requires a wide and alert focus. In contrast, the appropriate focus for a free throw is narrow. The athlete should pay no attention to other players, the crowd noise, or anything except the ball and the basket. For many players it is difficult to suddenly make this radical shift in focus. They remain aware of and are distracted by the other players, the fans behind the basket, and the crowd noise. The second factor is that free throws involve a change from a team emphasis to an individual effort. Team sports and individual sports require different approaches and thought processes. Hypnosis helps players achieve both the focus and the type of effort needed for 100 percent success.

Identifying a Successful Technique

My procedure for this correction is straightforward. I first watched Beth shoot several free throws. I noted the steps and rhythm she used when her shots went in. She was successful with several routines, so I chose the one with the least number of motions. I established a count to define the rhythm of one of Beth's successful throws. It was as follows:

> 5—look at the basket
>
> 4—dribble
>
> 3—dribble
>
> 2—look at the basket again
>
> 1—shoot

It is important not to prescribe the player's procedure or rhythm. The count must coincide with the player's successful pattern. It is interesting to me that many players have no consistent free throw pattern and are often unaware of the pattern used in their successful throws.

Demonstrating the Power of Self-Talk

At this point I used a muscle-testing exercise to demonstrate the power of self-talk. I describe this demonstration in chapter 9, "Gaining Inner Strength." Basically, it shows how much more strength players generate when they say, "I will make this free throw," rather than, "I hope to make this throw," or, "I'll try to make this throw." After Beth saw the increase in strength when she affirmed she would make the free throw, I suggested that she say, "I will make this throw" before each attempt.

Tying Induction to the Successful Procedure

After I had determined the count for the successful pattern, I worked with Beth in a quiet place, separate from the court. After an induction and deepening, I made several posthypnotic suggestions. The first suggestion was to establish a rapid reinduction cue. Typically, I suggest that the player will be able to go into a trance when I count from five down to one. I matched the pace of this count with the count of her successful free throw pattern. (Beth's free throw pattern fit a five count. Usually a player's motions include a few dribbles, a look at the basket, and a throw. Some players add other motions such as shuffling the feet into position, twirling the ball, and so on. If a player has more steps in her procedure, I would have a longer count.) I also told Beth that when I counted up from one to five, she would come out of the trance. I had her come in and out several times to establish the five to one count as a way to enter a trance rapidly.

The second series of suggestions attached the counting of the free throw pattern to the count for entering a trance. I went over Beth's procedure for her successful free throws and attached the count to her free throw procedure by suggesting that we together count from five down to one as she imaged a free throw and went into a trance. She had no problem experiencing a kinesthetic reaction as we counted and imaged her free throw. As she established this light trance, I suggested that in this trance, she would become totally focused on the basket, see nothing but the basket, hear nothing, and know the ball would go into the basket cleanly. I told her that the trance would end when she saw the ball arching downward from the throw.

Teaching Self-Hypnosis

As soon as this free throw procedure was established in the hetero-induced trance, I taught her to self-induce a trance using the same five to one count. Because self-hypnosis is difficult for some individuals, achieving this sometimes takes a second session, but Beth was able to self-induce a trance rapidly. After she could self-induce a trance, I asked her to again image a free throw by first saying, "I will make this throw," then starting the count, timing her actions with the count developed earlier. I emphasized that this procedure would assure a successful shot. This imaging was rehearsed several times until Beth felt comfortable with the self-induced trance and the imaging. We did all this away from the court.

On-Court Practice

My usual test of success is that the player can use the technique to make 10 successive free throws. Sometimes this is successful the first time the player attempts the shots; other times, I again hetero-induce a trance and reinforce the suggestions and reimaging. Then I ask the player to self-induce the trance and make the 10 free throws.

When Beth and I transferred our action back to the basketball court, I asked Beth to stand at the free throw line, take the ball from me as though from the referee, and perform what she imaged earlier, that is, to say, "I will make this shot." She then would start the count, go into a trance with the count, and make the free throw. Beth made seven shots in a row, then missed one. We went off to the side, I rehypnotized her and reinforced the suggestions and she self-induced a trance and im-aged making several shots. Then Beth went out and made the 10 in a row. She wanted to continue to see how many she could make. I re-minded her that all she ever had to do in a game was make two in a row, but to go ahead now and see what she could do. She missed the 16th shot. When she was demonstrating her free throw technique at the beginning of our session, she was making less than half her throws.

Some players require several sessions before making 10 in a row. When the player does not make 10 in a row, I repeat and reinforce the suggestions in hetero-hypnosis several times as necessary. If a player requires several reinforcing sessions, it is useful to take a short time-out, take the player aside for a few minutes, and discuss anything ex-cept the free throws. The mental effort required in this procedure is greater than it appears at first, and a few moments of relaxation can help in achieving success.

After Beth had made her 15 in a row, I asked her in a trance to set a target for the free throw percentage in games for the first month of play, then for the rest of the season. Usually the percentage will be above 90 percent. If it is not, I encourage the player to set a target in this range. Beth set a target of 99 percent. (Since she was not likely to get 100 free throw opportunities, this was a clever target. It allowed for a miss, but also showed an expectation of making all shots.) I suggested that she image the future time when she has achieved this percentage, perhaps looking at a stat sheet a month into the season and at the end of the season. I encouraged her to image and describe the feelings that would accompany this achievement, most importantly her personal feelings, but also the coach and team approval and the recognition by anyone else important to her. She immediately thought of her parents, who lived in town and attended every basketball game. I discuss this part of the technique in the section on "Memories of the Future" in chapter 6. I stressed to Beth the importance of practicing this routine on her own every day for a few days, then several times per week to thoroughly establish the routine in her mind and body.

Therapy Results

Beth decided that her goal was a shot that went in without touching the rim, a swish. A shot that touched the rim was a slight failure. Beth was able to use the procedure in the regular games. After the first month of play, when she missed no free throws (a swish percentage of 65), several other members of the team decided the procedure was for them too. During the rest of the season she missed only one free throw and had a swish percentage of about 70.

Why the Procedure Works

The player accomplishes several important mental changes by this procedure. First, she will be able to go immediately from the wide focus appropriate in regular play to the narrow focus appropriate for a free throw. Second, she establishes a degree of inner strength and confidence, which will contribute to the success of the free throw. Third, the player will be able to change from a team focus to an independent focus. Usually players who follow the procedure in games will more than cut in half the percentage of missed shots. Although not every throw will be successful, often the percent made will be above 90.

Several players who I have helped with this technique find that the focus for free throws is also appropriate for three-pointers. The focus on the center of the rim and the confidence improves those shots as much as it improves the free throws.

This procedure uses techniques from several chapters of the book. In addition to the obvious imaging techniques, this procedure incorporates the self-talk described in chapter 9, "Gaining Inner Strength," the focusing techniques from chapter 8, "Eliminating Distractions," as well as goal setting and future memories from chapter 6, "Building Motivation With Goals."

FINAL THOUGHTS

In this final chapter, I will tie up some loose ends—thoughts that did not fit elsewhere but might be useful to those considering using hypnosis with athletes. Among the notes I kept for an earlier book that I wrote, I instituted a folder labeled, "Rocks and Gems." In the folder I put a variety of ideas; some were useless rocks and others nice gems. That is what this chapter is, rocks and gems, but I hope mostly gems.

Thoughts on Hypnosis

Hypnosis, like any powerful tool, has potential for good and for harm. Most of this book has stressed the effectiveness of the technique, but therapists must also be aware of the hazards. We should not see hypnosis as either an all-powerful cure for any athlete's ailment or a dangerous weapon fraught with peril.

Ingredients for Success

It is important to note that hypnosis is, in itself, not a treatment. It is a technique that facilitates a variety of treatments, a technique that can make other treatments effective. The effectiveness depends upon both the hypnotist and the athlete. An effective hypnotherapist must have the expertise not only in hypnosis, but also in designing an appropriate way of dealing with the current concerns of the athlete and, most importantly, in handling any problems that might arise in the hypnotic trance.

The athlete must be at least somewhat susceptible to hypnosis. I have found few athletes who are not susceptible enough to enter a light trance, which is all I need for most of my work. It is more important for the athlete to have trust in the integrity and competence of the therapist. That is, the athlete must be both able and willing to benefit from hypnosis.

Hypnotic Responses

As you might expect, a person's responses in a trance are, in some interesting ways, different from normal responses. Getting used to these responses takes some familiarity with hypnosis.

A person in a trance seems to have trouble incorporating negative words. I rarely use negative words such as no, not, and never in a trance. An athlete who is told, "Do not get tense," is likely to focus on tenseness, and tenseness will be the result. It is better to say, "Stay smooth," and have the focus on smoothness. Similarly, it is more effective to tell a high jumper, "Aim for the open space above the bar" than to say, "Do not hit the bar." It is more effective to suggest to the athlete what *to do*, rather than what *not to do*. Describing what to avoid produces a focus on the unwanted behavior, and describing the desired behavior produces that behavior. As you may recognize, this applies to normal suggestions as well. For example, try hard right now *not* to think of an elephant!

It is considerably easier in a trance to decrease strength and performance than it is to improve them. Careless or unsophisticated remarks when made in a trance can damage performance.

Likewise, a person in a trance reacts to suggestions differently than when out of a trance. For example, individuals in a trance usually take posthypnotic suggestions much more literally than suggestions made when not in a trance. A story, which is probably apocryphal, illustrates this. A swimmer hoped to increase his speed. A hypnotist suggested that he would envision being chased by a shark in the pool. The swimmer took the suggestion literally, and although it did increase his speed in the first lap, at the end of that lap he leaped out of the pool to escape the threat. It takes some knowledge and experience of hypnosis to make posthypnotic suggestions that will bring the desired result—and only that result.

Psychic Dangers in Hypnosis

As mentioned earlier, the material in the unconscious becomes much more available in a trance. Included in the unconscious are memories and motivations that are in the unconscious because the person has trouble dealing with them. It is not unusual for a person in a trance to go back to some event and to experience what is called an abreaction. This is a highly charged emotional reaction to that event. These abreactions are possible whenever a subject is asked to regress to an earlier time or to examine the reasons for secondary gain from benign pain. Only therapists with solid graduate training in psychology should undertake work in these areas. A therapist trained in both hypnosis and in psychology can help the person deal with those abreactions should they emerge in a session. Some psychotherapists encourage these as a way of helping a person through a psychic problem. If they should emerge when the hypnotist is not appropriately trained, considerable damage might occur to the person's mental balance. This is probably the most dramatic of the problems that can damage a hypnotized person, but there are others, often related to the language cautions just discussed, but too many to cover here.

Hypnosis Training

This leads to considering what training is necessary before someone uses hypnosis. It is not difficult to learn how to help a person enter a trance. Learning that is the easiest part of hypnosis training. The much more difficult part is learning what to do to benefit the person in the trance.

The two most ethical organizations that offer training in hypnosis are the American Society for Clinical Hypnosis (ASCH) and the Society for Clinical and Experimental Hypnosis (SCEH). SCEH is more interested in research on hypnosis, and its requirements for membership are more restrictive than those of ASCH. The ASCH offers the most training opportunities, but its training and membership are restricted to appropriately licensed persons with doctoral degrees in dentistry, medicine, and psychology; persons holding masters degrees in social work, marriage and family counseling, and clinical or counseling psychology; and nurses holding masters degrees. It offers training to students in programs leading to these degrees. ASCH stresses the rule that you should not attempt any work with a person in a trance that you are not qualified to do with a person not in a trance.

ASCH offers programs in various parts of the country, usually scheduled Thursday through Sunday. ASCH offers certification in clinical hypnosis to candidates with 40 hours of acceptable workshop training, 20 hours of approved consultation, and two years of documented clinical use of hypnosis. Obviously, this organization regards learning hypnosis and certifying hypnotists as a serious undertaking. ASCH and SCEH believe that hypnosis by persons who are not properly trained can be a threat to the well-being of their subjects. This is why they restrict their training to those with the background to handle the problems that may emerge in a trance.

A variety of proprietary organizations offer training and certification in hypnosis. Some of these organizations are ethical and some are little better than diploma mills. The American Institute of Hypnotherapy (AIH), for example, offers weekend courses introducing the basics of hypnosis. The AIH courses are open to all who are willing to pay the registration fee, currently $295 for the 2 1/2 day course. Weekend participants who complete a test and send in $75 following the weekend receive a Certificate in Hypnotherapy from the American Board of Hypnotherapy—an agency owned by AIH. One can follow these weekend programs by AIH, then complete some brief home-study plans that lead to more advanced hypnosis skills and a variety of doctoral degrees that are awarded by the American Pacific University—a proprietary institution owned by the same person who owns AIH.

There is no universally recognized certification in hypnotherapy. As far as I have found out, no university with the usual American accreditation offers a major or concentration in hypnotherapy, although many American universities offer individual courses in hypnosis as a part of medical or psychology programs.

Learning and using hypnosis is a serious undertaking. Before enrolling in any program, I would advise reviewing the experience of several trustworthy individuals who have participated in the program. The certificates that these agencies sell have little value except as wall decoration, although I must admit that some make elaborate, impressive wall decorations!

Hypnosis, then, is a two-edged sword. In unsophisticated hands it can cause problems, but its use by skilled hands can help an athlete control the level of arousal, make imagery more vivid and helpful, set and visualize goals, maintain an appropriate focus in practices and in competitions, improve self-confidence, and even reduce pain and promote healing. All these skills can improve the self-efficacy of the athlete, which empowers the athlete to perform at his or her best in competition.

Thoughts for Nonhypnotists

Although I have discussed the various ways to develop mental skills using hypnosis, I should add that coaches and trainers can help athletes develop these skills *without* a deep hypnotic trance. Many techniques described in this book can be effective when the athletes are in a light trance, or simply relaxed. Coaches and athletes who want to develop the mental skills but do not have extensive training in psychology can take advantage of the power of suggestions outlined in this book. The relaxation exercises of Suinn, Jacobson, and Benson will produce a relaxed state and a susceptibility to suggestion.

Placebo Effect

A caution of a different type concerns the placebo effect. The experience of hypnosis is an exciting and dramatic experience for most people. If they believe that this technique will help them, it is likely that it will. Although the placebo effect can be helpful, it is difficult to separate it from the effect of the hypnosis. In working with an athlete, I exhibit complete confidence in the power of hypnosis to bring about the changes we seek. It seems self-defeating to start a session if the athlete and the psychologist think that hypnosis might not help. Success is more likely if the hypnotist can convey to the athlete that hypnosis will help with the problem. Sometimes when an athlete is in a trance, I say that I am wondering whether some specific suggestion might work, but I do this only when I am certain that the athlete is determined to have the suggestion work. That is, I am sure the athlete will choose to have the suggestion work and thus believe that we will realize the desired effect. The athlete's confidence will empower the suggestions.

I once submitted an article for publication with the statement admitting that when I viewed my therapy from a scientific point, I could not always separate the effect of hypnosis from the placebo effect. I added, "from a practical standpoint, it does not matter since the technique works." An anonymous reviewer of my article objected to this and wrote, "This issue is more than a scientific issue. It also involves ethical, moral and legal issues." Without denying that it would be desirable scientifically to be able to separate the two factors, I do not feel it is unethical, immoral, or illegal to capitalize on the placebo effect. In practice, it is foolish not to. When I use hypnosis, I draw on the placebo effect as much as possible, and I do not worry about those problems in so doing. I do not concern myself with how much improvement is due to hypnosis and how much is due to a placebo effect. My interest is in empowering the athlete.

Thoughts on Mental Training

Much of this book has dealt with the mental skills that an athlete needs for peak physical performance. There are other aspects of life that deserve some mention.

An Athlete Is More Than a Bunch of Muscles

In the effort to improve performance, I would urge you to give the prime attention to the athlete as an individual. Coaches and sport psychologists should be interested in helping an athlete as a person beyond helping athletic performance. Sports are only one aspect of any person's life, and other factors deserve the athlete's attention. Even for the elite athlete, there will be life after and in addition to the athletic career. The athlete should keep in mind some larger personal goals. You should encourage and help an athlete who has no goals or interests outside of athletics to develop some.

This is particularly true of collegiate athletes. Although many college and university football and basketball players hope for a professional career, few will make their living as athletes after graduation, and most of those careers last only a few years. You can encourage some larger career and personal goals. Even if the goal is the pros, the athlete should anticipate and prepare for a life after that. A coach or psychologist with a good relationship with an athlete can help that person consider what will happen when the athletic part of the life is over.

Have Fun

Another personal bias is that I feel sports must be fun. An athlete who does not enjoy practices and competition should be helped to regain the fun of the sport. As mentioned earlier, Gallwey (1998) urges that every time an athlete performs in practice or in competition, fun should be present. If he or she cannot do this, at least most of the time, the athlete should probably get out of the competition. Enjoyment not only enhances performance but contributes to personal and team morale.

Because a lot of my work (I should say my fun) is with high school and college athletes, I regularly find athletes who are in the sport because of parental pressure or because they think their social status depends upon being on the team. Rarely do these athletes become the top performers. Participation when the athlete is not enjoying the sport is likely to keep him or her from the best performances and from finding an area in which life can be more interesting and productive. I once taught at a college where the football team had not won a game for two years. Outsiders wondered how the players' morale could hold up after such a record. The coach, and I believe he was a good coach, knew the reason for the team was the players' enjoyment. He helped them to play hard but also to enjoy the game. The school had no athletic scholarships so the players were playing for the fun of the game. The coach admitted it would probably be more fun if they won once in a while, but the losses could not take the fun out of playing the game. I'm sure these players benefited more from football than players in schools where a loss takes all the pleasure out of the sport. The ability of this coach to take mediocre players (don't tell them I called them this!) and enable them to continue to have fun from the game made me label this coach as truly great. I am sure that some athletes play their game in order to win, but the best athletes try to win in order to play the game.

My Postscript

I have had a lot of fun with hypnosis. It is not the sort of fun that you associate with a stage hypnotist creating belly laughs when an audience sees the subjects cavorting about with embarrassing behavior. It is the deep enjoyment that comes from helping other people become able to do the things that they want to do.

I wish for the reader a lot of that fun and much success with this wonderful tool called hypnosis.

APPENDIX: REDUCING FEAR IN A RELUCTANT ATHLETE

THERE LIVES MORE FAITH IN HONEST DOUBT,
BELIEVE ME THAN IN HALF THE CREEDS.

TENNYSON, "IN MEMORIUM"

Occasionally I find an athlete who seems to want help but is reluctant to be hypnotized. Many who might benefit from hypnosis associate it with manipulative stage hypnotists or treacherous movie villains and have no wish to risk being put in a similar situation. A dialogue such as the following may help take care of his or her fears. This dialogue might suggest that I feel hypnosis is always the best technique to use. It isn't. Often nonhypnotic interventions are more useful; for this dialogue, however, accept that hypnosis is the most appropriate technique.

I had worked with several other members of Murph's swim team, and Murph had seen how hypnosis helped his teammates. He obviously had mixed feeling about working with me. His teammates and the coach encouraged him to try hypnosis because he was having problems with his flip turns. He was concerned with his flip turn but also about being hypnotized. The following dialogue applies to Murph's flip turn, but it is equally applicable to many other situations.

TALKING THROUGH THE FEARS

Murph: I really need help with my flip turns, but I'd rather have you help me without using hypnosis. Do you have to hypnotize me?

DL: No, I don't have to hypnotize you, Murph. I can use some other technique, but I think hypnosis might be more effective. Let's talk about hypnosis a bit. You can ask me questions about it, and if you decide you want me to use some other technique, I will do so. What do you know about hypnosis?

Embarrassment Issues

Murph: Well, I have seen those hypnotists on a stage, and they make people do foolish, embarrassing things. I don't want to go around flapping my arms like a chicken or making a fool of myself.

DL: That is not what I do with hypnosis. The stage hypnotist is up there to entertain an audience by using volunteers. I use hypnosis to help you do what you want to do. I'm not interested in making you do anything you wouldn't want to do, and there aren't any spectators here to watch us.

Control Issues

Murph: I just don't like the idea of having anyone controlling me, having the kind of power over me that those stage hypnotists have.

DL: Control is a tricky thing. When you are in a classroom with a good teacher, or when you listen to a good coach, are they controlling you?

Murph: Not really, I am still in control and can do whatever I want.

DL: Yes, you can do what you want, but you don't do whatever you want. You let the teacher or the coach determine what you do, or maybe I could say you want to do what they are controlling you to do. At any rate, you are allowing them to control you. You are conforming to, that is, you are being controlled by, the procedures and discipline of the situation.

Murph: Yes, I suppose I am, but I'm aware of what is going on, and I can quit when I want to. In hypnosis I'm just helpless.

DL: That is a misconception about hypnosis. All during the trance you will be aware of what is going on, and afterward you will remember what we did.

Memory Issues

Murph: When the guys came off the stage, they didn't seem to remember what they did.

DL: That is usually true. Those hypnotists suggest amnesia as part of the show. Maybe they want to get the people to buy the tapes of the show and make some more money. At any rate, I don't think that is ethical, and I want you to remember what we did in the trance.

Murph: OK, but what about the control?

DL: To learn anything from a good teacher or coach, you have to allow yourself to be controlled. Hypnosis is a form of control. The control is a little more obvious than the control of a coach, but even in hypnosis, you can decline any suggestion that I will make.

Murph: I guess I do let others control me. Maybe it is necessary for me to learn from a teacher or a coach, but they don't seem to have that much control. The control of a hypnotist seems too much.

DL: It certainly is more obvious, but does being more obvious mean you can't allow it? Just remember that any control I use will be designed to help you become a faster swimmer.

Murph: Can I really refuse a suggestion you make when I am in a trance? If so, how to I do it?

DL: If I make a suggestion you don't want to comply with, you will simply reject it and not respond to it. In a trance you are aware of what is going on, and you still retain a substantial degree of control.

Murph: If that is true, how is it that the stage hypnotist makes people do such ridiculous things when he has them in a trance? I don't think those people want to be doing those silly things. They look and act like they are completely under his control. I've never seen anyone on the stage refuse to do what the hypnotist suggests.

DL: Those people know in general what they are getting into when they volunteer. They volunteer knowing that they will be asked to do some silly but, they hope, rather harmless things, and they have decided to relinquish this control to the hypnotist. I wouldn't volunteer to look that silly, and you probably wouldn't either.

Murph: You're right, I sure wouldn't.

DL: If the hypnotist should ask them to do anything that would be harmful to them or against their moral standards, they would simply not accept the suggestions.

Danger Issues

Murph: How do you know they would not do something against their moral standards or harmful to them?

DL: That's a good question. We don't know that for sure, but in my experience and that of many others, people do reject the suggestions they feel they should reject. If they react negatively to a suggestion, they come out of a trance immediately.

Murph: Why doesn't someone do research to find out for sure whether this is true?

DL: Such an experiment would violate the firmly held principles of ethical research. Psychological researchers today are conscious of ethical principles, and one principle is that you cannot ask a participant in the research to do something that would harm that participant or anyone else. Thus you cannot hypnotize someone and ask that person to do something immoral or something that would harm that person or anyone else. So you cannot run an experiment in which you ask the person to do something that would be harmful.

I have heard about an experiment in which a hypnotized person was asked to stick his hand down into a cage where there were some live rattlesnakes. The top of the cage appeared to be open, but there was a glass that would keep the person from contacting the snakes. The hypnotized person did attempt to reach into the cage but the glass stopped his hand.

Afterward he was asked why he risked putting his hand into the cage. He said he trusted the hypnotist-experimenter, and he knew that he would not be asked to reach his hand in if there were any danger in it.

At any rate, I won't ask you to do anything that is at all dangerous to you. Do you have any other questions or concerns?

Religious Issues

Murph: I have one funny question.

DL: Go ahead and ask it.

Murph: Well, a friend of mine says his minister says the Bible says hypnotism is the work of the devil, and he was glad I didn't let you work with me when you worked with other guys on the team. He says hypnotism is against the Bible and that some bad things can happen if you are in a trance. Why does he say that?

DL: Well, first, the Bible does not say anything about hypnosis. Hypnotism was not a concept recognized when the Bible was written, or even when the King James version of the Bible was published. Hypnosis was not identified as a distinct phenomenon until the late 1700s. Many ancient cultures did use something that appears much like hypnosis. Trance work seems to have been used in the ancient Greek temple at Delphi, by ancient Egyptians, and by other societies, including the Hebrews of the Bible. There are statements in the Bible condemning the use of rituals of heathen people, and some fundamentalist Christians take that as forbidding hypnosis.

Murph: If they didn't have a word for it, what makes you think they used it?

DL: The Biblical references to deep sleeps or trances suggest to me that hypnosis, or something much like it, was familiar to the Biblical writers.

Murph: Where do those terms appear?

DL: They appear rather early. Genesis 1 says God put Adam in a deep sleep when he took out a rib to form Eve. This suggests to me that the Genesis writer was familiar with the anesthetic power of hypnosis. The power of hypnosis to ease pain was an early use and is still an important use of hypnosis.

Murph: Where else does the Bible talk about hypnosis or something that might be hypnosis?

DL: The Bible has several other references to trances—two in Numbers (24:4 and 24:16) and three in Acts (10:10, 11:5, and 22:17). In all five events, something good happened, usually a vision or revelation of God's will for that person. None could be construed as a bad occurrence. The creation of a woman, for example, was, in my view, a particularly good thing. The descriptions of the healing accomplished by Peter (Acts 3:4) and by Paul (Acts 14:8) also suggest that they used some sort of trance.

Murph: Are you sure that these references apply to hypnosis?

DL: No, I'm not sure, because I wasn't there, but hypnosis seems to me a valuable technique—not at all the work of the devil. The texts that condemn hypnosis as well as the ones that support its use are all interpretations. Because the Biblical writers did not have a term for hypnosis, all the pro and con proof texts are suspect. What I suggest here is also just my interpretation.

Murph: I guess that answers my question. Because the Biblical writers did not have a term for it, we can't be sure whether they used it or condemned it, or even knew what it was. I guess I don't need to be concerned on that issue.

DL: That's my feeling on the Biblical problem. I have found hypnosis to be so useful that it is hard for me to see it as an evil ritual. Do you have any other questions, Murph?

Coming Out Issues

Murph: Well, I do have another one. What happens if a person gets stuck in a trance and can't come out?

DL: There is no danger of that. If I left you alone while you were in a trance, you would either come out of it on your own quickly or you would fall into a normal sleep. Further, one of the things I will teach you is how you can bring yourself out of a trance any time you want to do so.

Murph: You'll be sure to teach me that?

DL: Yes. I will do that and allow you to practice doing it early in our session.

Final Assurance

DL: Any other questions?

Murph: Do you really think that being hypnotized could help me with my flip turns?

DL: Yes, I do.

Murph: You won't make me cluck like a chicken?

DL: I believe I can improve your flip turns, but I cannot guarantee it. I have no reason at all to make you into a chicken and a good reason not to. If you do act like a chicken when I am working with you, you'll probably go tell all the other team members, then they will be reluctant to let me help them. So, all I'm interested in doing is helping you and your teammates become better swimmers.

Murph: OK. I guess I don't have anything to lose by being hypnotized and maybe something to gain. What do I have to do?

DL: You have to be willing to follow a few suggestions. I cannot hypnotize you without your cooperation, so let's go ahead. Ready?

Murph: Ready as I'll ever be. Let's go.

GLOSSARY

diaphragm breathing—Using the full capacity of the lungs by contracting the diaphragm as well as expanding the ribs.

external imagery—Imagery in which the imager sees the activity without feeling a participation in the activity. The imager sees as though a third person is doing the activity.

fractionation—Deepening a trance by having the hypnotized person come in and out of a trance several times.

hetero-hypnosis—Hypnosis facilitated by a hypnotizer (contrast with self-hypnosis).

imagery—A person, in or out of a trance, sees or feels an activity. Sometimes called visualization, imagery suggests involving the kinesthetic, auditory, and emotional senses as well as the visual.

induction—The process of helping a person enter a trance.

internal imagery—Imagery in which the imager feels actual participation in the activity (contrast with external imagery).

kinesthetic—Applies to muscles.

outcome goal—A target to perform at a certain level in a competition (see performance goal).

performance goal—A target to achieve a specified improvement in one's own performance (see outcome goal).

placebo—A treatment that has no known effect but may result in a benefit because the patient believes the treatment will be effective.

reinduction—Reentering a trance.

secondary gain—A benefit realized, often unconsciously, from an illness or injury that prolongs the symptoms of the illness.

self-hypnosis—A person enters a trance without the help of another person (contrast with hetero-hypnosis).

self-talk—The internal monologue as one talks to oneself.

REFERENCES

Bandura, A. (1986). *Social foundations of thought and action: A social cognitive theory.* Englewood Cliffs, NJ: Prentice Hall.

Barber, J. (1996). *Hypnosis and suggestion in the treatment of pain: A clinical guide.* NY: Norton.

Benson, H. (1975). *The relaxation response.* New York: Morrow.

———. (1987). *Your maximum mind.* New York: Times Books.

———. (1996). *Timeless healing: The power and biology of belief.* New York: Scribner.

Brown, W.A. (1997, September/October). The best medicine. *Psychology Today, 30,* 5, 56-60, 80-82.

Cox, R. (1994). *Sport psychology: Concepts and applications.* Dubuque, IA: Brown and Benchmark.

Crasilneck, H.B., and J.A. Hall. (1985). *Clinical hypnosis: Principles and applications* (2nd ed.). Orlando, FL: Grune & Stratton.

Csikszentmihalyi, M. (1990). *Flow: The psychology of optimal experience.* New York: Harper & Row.

Eisenberg, D. (1985). *Encounters with Qi: Exploring Chinese medicine.* New York: Penguin Books.

Ellis, A., and M. Bernard. (1985). *Clinical applications of rational emotive therapy.* New York: Plenum Press.

Fazey, J., and L. Hardy. (1988). The inverted-U hypothesis: A catastrophe for sport psychology? *British Association of Sport Sciences Monograph No. 1.* Leeds: The National Coaching Foundation.

Feltz, D.L., and D.M. Landers. (1983). The effects of mental practice on motor skill learning and performance: A meta-analysis. *Journal of Sport Psychology, 5,* 25-57.

Gallwey, W.T. (1998). *The inner game of golf.* (Revised ed.) New York: Random House.

Gould, D., and N. Damarjian. (1996). Imagery training for peak performance. In J.L. Van Raalte and B.W. Brewer (Eds.), *Exploring sport and exercise psychology.* Washington, DC: American Psychological Association.

Gould, D., L. Petlichkoff, J. Simons, and M. Vevera. (1987). Relationship between competitive state anxiety inventory—2 subscales and pistol shooting performance. *Journal of Sport Psychology, 9,* 33-42.

Hammond, D.C. (1981). *The serenity place.* Salt Lake City: University of Utah School of Medicine.

Hanin, Y.L. (1980). A study of anxiety in sports. In W.F. Straub (Ed.), *Sport psychology: An analysis of athlete behavior* (pp. 236-249). Ithaca, NY: Mouvement Press.

————. (1995). Individual zones of optimal functioning (IZOF mode 1: An idiographic approach to performance anxiety). In K.P. Henschen and W.F. Strand (ed.), Sport psychology: An analysis of athlete behavior (3rd ed., pp. 103-118). Longmeadow, MA: Mouvement Press.

Hartland, J. (1971). Further observations on the use of ego-strengthening techniques. *American Journal of Clinical Hypnosis,* 14, 1-8.

Highlen, P.S., and B.B. Bennett. (1983). Elite divers and wrestlers: A comparison between open- and closed-skill athletes. *Journal of Sport Psychology,* 5, 390-409.

Hilgard, E.R., and J.R. Hilgard. (1975). *Hypnosis in the relief of pain.* Los Altos, CA: William Kaufman.

Huang, C.A., and J. Lynch. (1992). *Thinking body, dancing mind.* New York: Bantam Books.

Hughes, J.C., and A.E. Rothovius. (1996). *The world's greatest hypnotists.* New York: University Press of America.

Hunter, M. (1987). *Psych yourself in!: Hypnosis and health.* West Vancouver, BC: Seawalk Press.

Ievleva, L., and T. Orlick. (1991). Mental links to enhanced healing: An exploratory study. *The Sport Psychologist,* 5, 1, 25-40.

Jacobson, E. (1929). *Progressive relaxation.* Chicago: University of Chicago Press.

————. (1938). *Progressive relaxation* (2nd ed.). Chicago: University of Chicago Press.

————. (1976). *You must relax.* New York: McGraw-Hill.

Kirsch, I., and S.J. Lynn. (1995). The altered state of hypnosis: Changes in the theoretical landscape. *American Psychologist,* 50, 846-858.

Krane, V. (1993). A practical application of the anxiety-athletic performance relationship: The zone of optimal functioning hypothesis. *The Sport Psychologist,* 7, 113-126.

Landers, D. (1980). The arousal-performance relationship revisited. *Research Quarterly for Exercise and Sport,* 51, 77-90.

Liggett, D.R. (2000). Enhancing imagery through hypnosis: A performance aid for athletes. Accepted for publication in the *American Journal of Clinical Hypnosis.*

Liggett, D.R., and S. Hamada. (1993, January). Enhancing the visualization of gymnasts. *American Journal of Clinical Hypnosis,* 35, (3), 190-197. (A shorter version of this paper appears as Liggett, D.R., and S. Hamada. [1992, March]. Hypnosis: A key to effective visualization. *U.S. Gymnastics Technique,* 12, 20-22.)

Louganis, G., and E. Marcus. (1995). *Breaking the surface.* New York: Random House.

Lutz, M., and D.R. Liggett. (1998). Supercharging visualization for wildwater racing. *Canoe and Kayak Racing News,* 1, 3. (U.S. Canoe and Kayak Team Official Publication)

Martens, R. (1982). Imagery in sport. In M.L. Howell and A.W. Parker (Eds.), Proceedings of the Australian sports medicine federation international conference. Vol. 8. *Sports medicine: Medical and scientific aspects of elitism in sport,* 213-230.

Martin, K.A., and C.R. Hall. (1995). Using imagery to enhance intrinsic motivation. *Journal of Sport and Exercise Psychology*, 17, 59-67.

McClelland, D. (1955). Some social consequences of achievement motivation. In M. Jones (Ed.), *Nebraska symposium on motivation*. Lincoln: University of Nebraska Press.

Montana, J., and R. Weiner. (1997). *Art and magic of quarterbacking*. New York: Holt.

Moyers, W.B. (1993). *Healing and the mind*. New York: Doubleday.

Nideffer, R.M. (1992). *Psyched to win*. Champaign, IL: Human Kinetics.

Raglin, J.S., and P.E. Turner. (1993). Anxiety and performance in track and field athletes: A comparison of the inverted-U hypothesis with the zone of optimal functioning theory. *Personality and Individual Differences*, 14, 163-171.

Russell, B., and T. Branch. (1979). *Second wind: The memoirs of an opinionated man*. New York: Random House.

Ryan, E.D., and J. Simons. (1983). What is learned in mental practice of motor skills: A test of the cognitive-motor hypothesis. *Journal of Sport Psychology*, 5, 419-426.

Seligman, M. (1990). *Learned optimism: How to change your mind and your life*. New York: Pocket Books.

Shor, R.E., and E.C. Orne. (1962). *Harvard group scale of hypnotic susceptibility*. Palo Alto, CA: Consulting Psychologists Press.

Spiegel, H., and D. Spiegel. (1978). *Trance and treatment: Clinical uses of hypnosis*. Washington, DC: American Psychiatric Press.

Spielberger, C.D. (1983). *Manual for the state-trait anxiety inventory*. Palo Alto, CA: Consulting Psychologists Press.

Suinn, R.M. (1976). Body thinking: Psychology for Olympic champs. In R.M. Suinn (Ed.), *Psychology in sports: Methods and applications* (pp. 306-313). Minneapolis: Burgess. (This article also appears in Suinn, R.M. (1976, July). *Psychology Today*, 38-43.)

———. (1993). Imagery. In R. Singer, M. Murphey, and L. Tennant, *Handbook of research on sport psychology* (pp. 492-510). New York: Macmillan.

SyberVision. (1996). Tapes may be obtained from SyberVision, Inc., One Sansome Street, Suite 810, San Francisco, CA 94104. Information available from **www.sybervision.com.**

Tenenbaum, G., M. Bar-Eli, J.R. Hoffman, and R. Jablonovski. (1995). The effect of cognitive and somatic psyching-up techniques on isometric leg strength performance. *Journal of Strength and Conditioning Research*, 9, 3-7.

Unestål, L.-E. (1986a). *Contemporary sport psychology*. Orebro, Sweden: Veje.

———. (1986b). The ideal performance. In L.-E. Unestål (Ed.), *Sport psychology in theory and practice*. Orebro, Sweden: Veje.

———. (1995). The application of inner mental training to sport and life. Unpublished Plenary Address at Frontiers of Hypnosis, Banff, Canada. May 6, 1995.

Weinberg, R.S., and D. Gould. (1999). *Foundations of sport and exercise psychology* (2nd ed.) Champaign, IL: Human Kinetics.

Weitzenhoffer, A.M., and E.R. Hilgard. (1959). *Stanford hypnotic susceptibility scale.* Palo Alto, CA: Consulting Psychologists Press.

Whitmark, B. (1998, May). Pushing the pain barrier: Mental strategies to keep training when your muscles say stop. *Muscle and Fitness, 58,* 5.

Yerkes, R.M., and J.D. Dodson. (1908). The relationship of strength of stimulus to rapidity of habit formation. *Journal of Comparative Neurology and Psychology, 18,* 459-482.

Index

About the Author

Donald R. Liggett is a retired professor of psychology and education and a hypnotherapist certified through the American Society for Clinical Hypnosis. He has worked with a wide variety of athletes, including powerlifters, basketball players, football kickers and receivers, gymnasts, wrestlers, hockey players, and cross country runners. He received his master's degree in experimental psychology and doctorate in international education and educational psychology from Stanford University. While teaching the psychology of hypnosis at Stanford, he became the first person to use hypnosis to improve the athletic performance of members of Stanford's gymnastics and football teams.

In 1997, Liggett was invited to teach sport psychology at the University of Malaya and to use hypnosis to help Malaysian athletes prepare for the 1998 Commonwealth Games. These efforts were rewarded when three of his athletes won medals—two gold and one bronze.

Liggett and his wife, Jeanne, live in Gig Harbor, Washington. In his free time he enjoys growing dahlias, downhill skiing, playing the piano, and traveling.

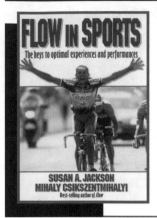
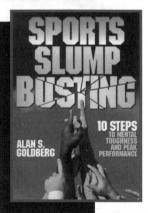